OLD ENGLISH CUSTOMS

OLD ENGLISH
CUSTOMS

ROY CHRISTIAN

DAVID & CHARLES
NEWTON ABBOT

ISBN 0 7153 5741 7

First published in 1966 by Country Life Limited
This edition published in 1972 by David & Charles Limited

Printed in Great Britain by
Redwood Press Limited, Trowbridge, Wiltshire
for David & Charles (Publishers) Limited
South Devon House Newton Abbot Devon

TO MY WIFE

Contents

Illustrations

ILLUSTRATIONS

ACKNOWLEDGMENTS TO PHOTOGRAPHERS

The author wishes to acknowledge the following photographers for supplying photographs used in his book.

Plates 1, 2, 3, 7, 21, 24, 25, 35, 46, 47, 61, 65, 67, 68, 79, 80, 81, 82, 85, 91, 104, 106, 108, 114, 115, 125, 126, Reece Winstone; 4, 5, 6, 37, 38, 39, 40, 41, 42, 43, 45, 51, C. Eric Brown; 8, 16, 18, 19, 127, *Yorkshire Evening Post;* 10, 11, 12, 27, 28, 128, Nicholas Horne; 9, 103, *Hampshire Chronicle;* 13, 14, 15, 17, Kathleen Mitchell; 20, 63, 98, 117, *The Guardian;* 22, The Mansell Collection; 31, 34, 55, *Kent Messenger;* 23, Cyril Lindley; 26, *Bedfordshire Times;* 30, 33, 56, 71, 74, 75, 78, 89, 101, 123, British Travel Association; 29, 32, 53, 59, 60, 64, 72, 83, 99, 100, 109, 124, *The Times;* 36, 52, 54, 57, 58, 66, 69, 73, 76, 77, 90, 93, 94, 96, 97, 102, 105, 107, 110, 111, 112, 116, 118, 121, 122, Radio Times Hulton Picture Library; 44, 87, Frank Rodgers; 48, 113, Raymonds News Agency; 49, 120, F. Leonard Jackson; 50, 119, *Guardian Journal;* 62, R. L. Palmer; 70, Barratts Photo Press Ltd; 84, United Press International Ltd; 86, *Northumberland Gazette;* 90, Topix; 92, Leeds Photopress; 95, Arthur Gaunt.

Acknowledgments

To thank individually all those who have helped in the writing of this book would be a monumental task, but it would be churlish not to mention my indebtedness to those who have written previously on old English customs, some of whom are listed in the bibliography. It would also be unpardonable if I failed to acknowledge collectively my gratitude to all those people who have so kindly and patiently answered my numerous enquiries, both verbally and in writing, and who have in many cases lent me documents and cuttings. I must especially thank Mr Frank Rodgers, who has given up so much precious time in his search for photographs to illustrate this book.

Introduction

'If you care to wait another ten minutes', said the woman verger in the church of St Mary, Wiveton, 'you'll be able to see an interesting little custom.'

Sheer chance had taken me into Wiveton church on that fine Saturday afternoon in July. I enjoy exploring churches, and those in Norfolk are among the most rewarding in all England. Wiveton, facing the still more imposing church at Cley across a mile or so of green meadows that had once been a tidal estuary, is typical of many in the county: light, airy and disproportionately large for the present size of its parish. It was the size of the church, standing back from the houses across a village green, that had attracted my attention and made me stop my car to explore. And it was while I was admiring the magnificent Perpendicular nave that the verger arrived, and after a brief conversation, extended her invitation, which I gladly accepted.

So I waited the ten minutes, and promptly at four o'clock the verger tolled one of the church bells, the 'charity bell'. Equally promptly the north door opened and two elderly ladies appeared, were handed two half-crowns each out of a blue bag and went out again. They were the first of twelve veteran residents of Wiveton who in due course arrived to receive 5s. each, as they did every Saturday afternoon at four o'clock, under the terms of a will made over four centuries ago.

The will was made by Ralph Greneway, 'citizen and Alderman of Lo'don', who died in 1558, as a memorial brass in the south aisle reveals. He was a member of the Grocers' Company, a wealthy merchant with extensive interests in Wiveton and Cley in the days when the two places were thriving ports. He was a great benefactor to the two parishes, and among his benefactions was the award of old-age pensions—long before the State had thought of them—for those residents of Wiveton who had reached 60 years of age.

The simple ceremony that I had just attended—the tolling of the charity bell and the paying out of the pensions—had been enacted week by week without a break for more than 400 years; it will continue to be performed, presumably, for much more than another 400 years. How many more customs, I asked myself as I drove away from Wiveton, have endured so long?

The answer is that there are a great many. Some are as little publicised as the one I had watched; others have been widely written about, photographed, filmed, broadcast and televised so that they are well known not only in England, but overseas as well. Some go back much further than the Wiveton custom; many have less practical application. Some indeed have long since lost their original point and are practised now simply because nobody wants to break with tradition.

The curfew bell is a good example of this. In the Middle Ages the curfew was rung every evening throughout Europe as a signal that fires should be damped down for the night and lights extinguished. It was a precaution against fire in days when most houses were built of timber, and indeed the word comes from the Old French *cuevrefu*, 'cover fire'.

William the Conqueror is said to have introduced the curfew to this country, though he may have done no more than tighten up existing regulations. The absolute ban on lights was lifted as early as 1103, and over the centuries the sound of the curfew bell was heard less often as the need for it diminished. Yet it is still rung in many towns and villages, in some places from Michaelmas to Lady Day, in others all the year round.

In Derbyshire, where several villages still preserve the custom, I asked a local bell-ringer why he continued to ring the curfew. He seemed surprised by the question, and paused thoughtfully before replying. 'Why?' he repeated at last. ' 'Cos we've allus done it, I suppose.' And then, as though conscious of the inadequacy of his reply, he added: 'Besides, all t'village sets t'watches by it'.

Yet it is doubtful if many of these villagers could explain the origin of the curfew custom. And that goes for a host of other country customs behind which lurk origins as old as the hills.

Who, for example, knows why the villagers of Shebbear, in North Devon, turn out on the evening of November 5th each year to walk in procession, the men armed with ropes and crow-bars, the women carrying

1. The Horn Dance held at Abbots Bromley, Staffordshire. This is the leader wearing Tudor costume and carrying huge reindeer antlers.

2. The dancers walk round country lanes for something like 20 miles with their heavy antlers. Here they are nearing Blithfield Hall.

3. Part of the Horn Dance taking place in the main road. On the left is the Hobby Horse, while Robin Hood, with his bow and arrow, is nearest to the camera.

4. The Horn Dance in progress at Blithfield Hall. The Hobby Horse, Robin Hood, Maid Marion and the Jester may be seen on the right of the picture.

5. Maid Marion—a man in disguise—is shown here with 'her' collecting ladle.

6. Hobby Horse rider. By pulling strings, he can make the 'horse's' mouth open and shut with a clacking noise.

7. Morris dancing has continued at Bampton, in Oxfordshire, for some 500 years. For over 60 years this fiddler has led the dancers, and his family before him, for 200 years.

8. Here are Leeds Morris dancers at the Wharfedale village of Burnsall. Most Morris dancers wear white shirts and trousers, with bright ribbons or garlands.

9. These are Hampshire Morris dancers.

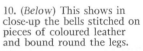

10. (*Below*) This shows in close-up the bells stitched on pieces of coloured leather and bound round the legs.

11, 12. Morris dancers in the Devon village of Widecombe-in-the-Moor. They have a hobby horse which appears in other traditional dances.

torches, candles and lanterns, to conduct a ceremony known as Turning the Devil's Boulder? Certainly the villagers themselves do not know, and most of them are reluctant to discuss it. But all have the uneasy feeling that if this huge stone that lies under an ancient oak tree near the church were not turned completely over once a year some disaster would strike the village and its inhabitants.

This belief has never been tested, for the simple reason that the boulder has been turned over every year for many centuries. Even during the war, when black-out regulations meant that the ceremony had to be carried out in total darkness and the usual ringing of the church bells at the beginning and end of the ceremony was also forbidden, the custom was strictly observed.

There are several theories about the origin of this stone-turning tradition. A legend has it that the Devil himself dropped the boulder when he was descending from Heaven to Hell. A more acceptable belief is that the stone was the centre of some long-forgotten pagan festival. Another possibility is that the stone marks a holy spot, perhaps associated with St Michael, patron saint of the parish church, a theory to which some credence is lent by the position of the stone near the entrance to the churchyard. It is more than likely that both these last two beliefs are true and that the stone, at one time the centre of pagan rites, became the scene of Christian worship before the parish church was built.

But two things are certain. One is that, despite the coincidence of date, the custom has no connection with Guy Fawkes, being of much earlier origin. The second is that the stone is completely alien to the locality, suggesting that it might have been placed in its present position for some ritualistic purpose.

This Shebbear custom is one of many in which the practice has survived 'the belief which gave it life', as A. H. Krappe puts it in *The Science of Folklore*. The rite has continued 'from man's innate conservatism, though the original reason or purpose had long been forgotten'. Nobody knows why the boulder has to be turned; it is now pure unreasoning superstition—a fear of the unknown—that prompts twelve powerful men to exert their strength on one night in each year to turn this huge stone completely over.

The people of Shebbear are by no means alone in clinging to superstition in this way. At Hallaton, Haxey, Abbots Bromley and many another place, as we shall see later on in this book, people preserve customs whose origins are completely forgotten, often inventing some spurious medieval origin to hide their ignorance of a much earlier tradition and to side-step the suggestion that they are perpetuating a superstition.

Sophisticated people may deplore the maintenance of such customs. In these days when England is trying to 'modernise' herself, to create a picture of a bustling, enterprising, industrialised country bursting with enthusiasm to export her teeming goods, the image that the British Travel Association puts out in its *New Yorker* advertisements of an Olde Worlde nation of morris dancers and maypoles on village greens is bad publicity. So the argument runs.

But those who argue in this way overlook the fact that some two and a half million overseas visitors come to Britain every year and spend nearly £350 million here. Many of them come to escape for a while from bustling, enterprising, industrialised countries and to see something of the history and pageantry that remain in these islands. So on economic grounds alone there is much to be said in favour of preserving our old customs.

Even if there were not, they would still go on. Our ancient customs have been dying for centuries. The 17th-century Puritans set out to exterminate them, but they only stunned, they did not kill, and the patient recovered. The 18th century saw no place for such unsophisticated revelry in an Age of Reason, and the gentry tried hard to abolish the observance of old feasts and customs on the grounds that they led to rowdiness and licence. Wordsworth, as Peter Opie has pointed out, 'thought himself born too late to take part in folk ritual'. Book VIII of *The Prelude* speaks of customs he had heard of as a boy; 'of maids at sunrise bringing in the may-bush from afar, of wreaths decking porches and church pillar, tales of the maypole and youths, each with his maid, issuing by annual custom, to drink the waters of some sainted well and hang it round with garlands.'

> But for such purpose, flowers no longer grow . . .
> The times too sage, perhaps too proud, have dropped
> These lighter graces; and the rural ways
> And manners which my childhood looked upon
> Were the unluxuriant produce of a life
> Intent on little but substantive needs.

The Victorians, more than a little shocked at the bawdiness lurking not far from the surface of many customs, saw no reason for their preservation in an age of enlightenment, though the cult of medievalism threw up a romantic counter-movement in the middle of the reign.

The coming of the railways seemed to herald the end of many customs.

By freeing the villagers from their isolation they would 'soon trample under foot and exterminate all traces of our beliefs and legends'. That was written in 1841 by W. J. Thomas, who coined the word 'folklore', and more than 50 years later P. H. Ditchfield, setting out to write such a book as this one, believed that Thomas's forecast had been fulfilled. '. . . The shriek of the engine has sounded the death-note of many once popular festivals. The railway trains began to convey large crowds of noisy towns-folk to popular rural gatherings and converted the simple rustic feasts into pandemoniums of vice and drunken revelry. Hence the authorities were forced to interfere, and to order the discontinuance of the festivals.'

Agricultural depression, Ditchfield declared, had killed many another rural custom. 'When poverty stands at the door, mirth and merriment are afraid to enter.' The increasing sophistication of the agricultural worker was another reason he advanced for the decline that he thought he saw of ancient customs. In fact he was decidedly fearful that there would be none left for him to write about by the time he had finished his book.

Nearly three-quarters of a century later, I have no such fears. True, many old customs did die in the 19th century, and two wars have since killed others. But many more are still regularly observed in the towns and villages of England. Some have changed greatly over the centuries, adapting their form to changing social and economic conditions. Others have been revived after lapsing for a while. But in the main they continue as they have done for centuries simply because they bring a great deal of pleasure to a great many people.

CHAPTER ONE

Traditional Dances

Abbots Bromley lies very close to the heart of England, both geographic-ally and in spirit. It is a long, straggling village, a pleasant mixture of red brick and black-and-white half-timber, that somehow hints at its earlier importance as a market-town and the centre of the former royal forest of Needwood. Birmingham, the Black Country and the Staffordshire Potteries are all less than an hour's run distant by car, but in atmosphere they are centuries away. Abbots Bromley belongs to a much older England where tradition persists, and it is not surprising to find it clinging enthusiastically to one of our oldest customs.

This is the unique Horn Dance, performed by men whose heads are half hidden by the antlers of reindeer (Plates 1–4). It is danced in Abbots Bromley on Wakes Monday—the first Monday after the first Sunday after September 4th. The Wakes is the successor to the old St Bartholo-mew's Fair, which used to be held on August 24th until the calendar was altered in 1752.

At 8.30 on the morning of Wakes Monday the dancers collect the six horns from the Hurst chapel in the parish church of St Nicholas, where they hang for the rest of the year. These are mounted on heads crudely carved in wood, with heavy wrought-iron fittings and stales by which they are carried. Three pairs are painted blue and the others white. The largest pair weighs $25\frac{1}{4}$ pounds and has a span of 39 inches. This pair is always carried by the leading dancer, but his colleagues have only slightly less weight to carry, the lightest pair of antlers weighing $16\frac{1}{2}$ pounds and the smallest span being 29 inches.

The origin of the horns is a mystery, but three main theories have been advanced to explain their presence in Abbots Bromley: either they were brought back from the Holy Land by an early member of the Bagot family from nearby Blithfield; or they were given by a 17th-century Lord Paget on his return from Constantinople, where he had been British Ambassador; or they came from reindeer brought by Norsemen to England in pre-Conquest times.

The Bagot theory is generally dismissed as pure legend, and, while Lord Paget undoubtedly imported some horns, the evidence is that they were elk horns and much heavier than the present set. It is believed that they were used for dances outside the parish, but were subsequently lost. So we are left with the Norse theory, which has the support of a former vicar of Abbots Bromley, the Rev. A. R. Ladell, whose booklet on the dance is on sale in the church. The visible evidence is that the carving of the heads is not later than the 16th-century. The horns themselves appear to be older, and if they are British they must be earlier than the 12th century, by which time the last reindeer in Scotland had died out, it is now thought.

There are also rival theories about the origin of the dance. One suggestion is that it commemorated the granting of hunting rights in the Needwood Forest in the Middle Ages. There is evidence from the cartulary of Burton Abbey that in 1125 the five men who farmed the manor of Abbots Bromley were granted grazing rights within the forest, but there is no mention of hunting rights, which were much more jealously guarded. Another theory is that the Horn Dance began no later than the reign of Henry VIII, those who hold this belief pointing to Maid Marian, the 'man-woman', Robin Hood and the hobby-horse, who now accompany the dancers, as popular characters of that time.

But there seems little doubt that these are later figures grafted on to a much earlier dance. For its beginnings we must surely go back to pre-historic pagan times, when primitive people dressed themselves in animal skins and mimed the behaviour of animals to ensure success in the chase. The nearest thing we have in this country to a cave painting is the engraving on bone that was found in a cave at Cresswell in Derbyshire. It depicts a man wearing horns very like the reindeer antlers of Abbots Bromley, and it is probably eight to ten thousand years old, certainly older than the earliest reference in the Bible to horns being worn by humans to typify strength.

The early Christian Church banned the 'devilish practice' of wearing animal skins and horns, but was forced to accept the dances themselves when they were purged of their uglier manifestations. And here at Abbots Bromley we have almost certainly a pagan rite, growing 'out of the enthusiasm and excitement which followed a successful hunt', as Mr Ladell puts it.

The dance itself is simple enough. First the six men with horns turn a circle; then the leader turns inwards and passes between the second and third dancers, the others following to form a complete loop. The dancers then face one another in two sets of three. Now comes the climax of the dance. With antlers raised as though to fight, the lines advance, passing left shoulder to left shoulder, the tips of their horns almost touching, and indeed occasionally making contact. After several repetitions the group resumes single file. The dance is then repeated at numerous strategic points over a fifteen-mile circuit of the hamlets and farms of the large parish, keeping the dancers at full stretch until 8 p.m.

Over the years the Horn Dance has acquired in addition to Maid Marian, with her curious collecting ladle, Robin Hood, with his bow and arrow, and the hobby-horse with clacking jaws, a jester with another collecting-box, a boy with a triangle and the musician whose accordion has displaced the traditional pipe and tabor (Plates 5 and 6).

The music itself is not old. Although four traditional tunes have been discovered in the last half-century or so, none of them is particularly ancient, and the dance today is usually performed to a modern dance tune.

The costumes, too, are comparatively recent. Before 1860 the dancers wore their own clothes decorated with ribbons and patches of cloth dyed to match the colour of the horns. Then some local ladies designed a costume which was worn at the celebrations for the restoration of the parish church. This innovation proved popular, and new costumes were provided by public subscription in 1892. The present ones, which were specially made in London in 1948, follow the cut and colour of their predecessors.

Only the most unbending of traditionalists could object to the introduction of the costumes, which have added a visual attraction to a dance that basically has not altered since it was first described in detail by Plot in 1686. Certainly the villagers themselves are determined to keep faith with tradition. This accounts for the purchase in 1964 of a duplicate set of six horns, insured for £100 each, to be used when the dancing takes place at functions outside Abbots Bromley, for tradition insists that the original horns must not be taken outside the parish.

Another tradition that is maintained is the remarkable link with the dance of the Folwell family, who claim to have been dancing the Horn

Dance in unbroken succession for 400 years, except during the Civil War and for a short period in the first World War, when the dance was suspended. The late Mr James Folwell, who gave up the leadership in 1962 at the age of 75, had been a dancer for 68 years, and he and his brother, Alfred George Folwell, had held the leadership between them for 41 years in succession. Now there are sons to continue the dynasty.

Other dancers come and go more rapidly, but there is no difficulty in obtaining the requisite dozen enthusiasts each year. They usually join as boys to dress up as Robin Hood or to play the triangle and then transfer to the horns when they are strong enough to carry them. They dance because they enjoy it, not because they are 'arty-crafty' people deliberately keeping up a tradition. The 1965 team included two pottery workers, a capstan lathe operator from an engineering works and a night watchman: a pretty fair cross-section of the village, in fact.

In recent years the Horn Dance has attracted increasing attention, and the coaches and cars bringing spectators in their thousands now provide an annual headache for the Staffordshire police. The danger is not that the dance may fade out, but that it may fall to the temptation to become commercialised, a temptation that has so far been firmly resisted.

The Morris Dance, too, is increasingly popular at the present time, especially in lowland England; north of the Derbyshire Peak it has keen competition from the closely-allied Sword Dance. There were in 1972 some 81 morris sides belonging to the Morris Ring, with the heaviest concentration in the West Midlands.

The origin of morris dancing is no clearer than that of the Horn Dance. It is probably another survival from the primitive past connected with food supply and the fertility of the soil, which gradually lost its original point in Christian times to become just another form of communal entertainment.

There is some conflict of opinion as to when it came to England. Some authorities put it as early as the time of the Crusades; others think it may have been brought here by soldiers who saw it performed in France during the Hundred Years' War. It is certainly not a native dance, and it probably came to this country from France, Flanders or Spain.

Because the dancers blackened their faces, the dance was thought by many people to have come from Morocco, the name being a corruption of 'Moorish', but this theory is unlikely, as the dance was performed outside the region of Moorish influence, and it was known long before the Moors invaded Spain. Blacking was intended, for superstitious reasons, to hide the identity of the dancers, a tradition that is still maintained by the mummers.

Morris dancing became extremely popular in England in Tudor times, both at court and in the towns and villages of the countryside. It was around that period that those popular characters of contemporary ballads, Robin Hood and Maid Marian—invariably, as at Abbots Bromley, a 'man-woman'—became attached to the dance, joining the older subsidiary figures, the fool, with his bladder on a stick, and the hobby horse.

All these figures have survived in morris sides to the present day. At Bampton, in Oxfordshire, where, it is claimed, the ring has existed for 500 years, there is an additional figure, a sword bearer whose decorated sword has a tin at its end containing a cake. Slices of the cake, which may be the modern equivalent of the head of a hunted animal, are distributed among the spectators and are supposed to bring good luck and husbands for the girls (Plate 7).

Generally there are eight dancers in a side, but the number varies slightly from place to place. They dance usually to traditional music supplied by a fiddle and an accordion, but sometimes a fife and tabor.

The dancers, all male, wear white cricket shirts and trousers with bright ribbons or garlands crossing back and chest (Plates 8–11). Bells are stitched on pieces of coloured leather and bound round the legs. Straw hats, gaily adorned with flowers, are the usual headgear, though cricket caps are worn by some sides and beflowered toppers are not unknown. The original object of the bright clothing was to assist the sun in its efforts to promote growth, just as the height reached by the dancers in their leaps was thought to influence the height to which the crops would grow.

Naturally, the dance was, and still is, performed chiefly out of doors in the early summer, particularly at May Day or Whitsun revels. It may be seen at its best in the annual Whitsun festivals at Bampton or near-by Headington, but you are likely to encounter morris dancers, especially in the West Midlands, at any summer weekend.

At Abingdon a Morris Mayor is elected annually on or near the Feast of St Edmund of Abingdon (June 19th) by the inhabitants of Ock Street. A wooden ballot box is placed on a table in the street and into it people place their ballot slips, which are then counted in the open before the candidates. Then the newly elected Mayor of Ock Street is 'danced in', first up and down Ock Street and later in different parts of the town, after which there is a celebration supper. The custom, which was revived in 1938 after an interval of 50 years, is said to have been begun in 1700 to commemorate a fight between the people of Ock Street and the rest of the town. This fight was followed by the roasting of an ox, whose horns—which gave their name to an inn, the Ock Street Horns—are still carried on a staff in front of the dancers.

Another unusual morris custom is observed at Bacup, in Lancashire, on Easter Eve. This is the Nutters Dance, in which the Britannia Coconut Dancers dance their way from one side of the town to the other, a distance of seven miles. No one knows why or when the custom began, but it was carried out by the Tunstead dancers before the Nutters were formed about 60 years ago. There are eight dancers and a 'whipper-in', who goes in front to whip away evil spirits, as well as two reserves and a concertina player, who is sometimes replaced by a local band. The dancers wear black clogs, with white stockings, black velvet breeches, red and white kilts, black jerseys and plumed white caps. On their hands and knees are fastened small discs of wood—the 'nuts'—and with these nuts the dancers beat a tattoo in chorus.

The dancers practise every week of the year, and I am told that interest in the dance is greater now than ever before and that there are plenty of young dancers waiting to fill any vacancies.

CHAPTER TWO

Folk Drama

Across the Pennines from Bacup lies the land of the Sword Dance. Miss Violet Alford, in her *Sword Dance and Drama*, published in 1962, found fourteen teams of sword dancers in places stretching from Grenoside and Handsworth, on the outskirts of Sheffield, almost to the banks of the Tweed. South of the Humber there seem to be no surviving teams, though some morris sides do perform a Sword Dance.

The fact that the Sword Dance in this country flourished chiefly inside the boundaries of the old Danelaw led to the belief that it was a survival of a Norse war dance. Sir Walter Scott propagated this theory, and his contemporaries, as eager to accept Norse origins as their 18th-century grandfathers had been to explain most customs as survivals from Classical mythology, unhesitatingly followed him. But in doing so they overlooked the popularity of the dance in Southern and Central Europe, outside the region of Norse influence.

Clearly the Sword Dance, closely related to the Morris Dance on the one hand and to the Mummers' and Plough Monday plays on the other, goes back much further than the Norse invasions in Europe. Tacitus saw it performed in Germany in the first century and was much impressed by the agility of the young men who flung themselves about among lethal spear-points and sword-blades. It is now accepted that the dance goes back deep into the roots of time and that it is a ritual dance concerned with the death of the Old Year and the birth of the New.

The basic steps of the dance are similar to those of the morris, but the handkerchiefs carried by the morris men are replaced by swords, either of steel with wooden handles or wholly of wood. The dance varies slightly from place to place, but there are fundamental differences between the Long Sword Dance of Yorkshire and the Short Sword, or Rapper, Dance of Northumberland and Durham. The Yorkshiremen, usually in teams of eight, use a sword three feet long or slightly more, whereas the five-men teams further north, whose steps have something in common with the Lancashire clog dance, favour the shorter, more flexible, two-handled rapper sword. Rapper sounds like a corruption of rapier, but in fact its origin goes further back than the first use of that light, slender sword.

The dress of the dancers also varies between one place and another. In general, the semi-military uniforms of the 19th century have been replaced by white tunics or shirts and white trousers, though the Flamborough team wear fishermen's jerseys of blue, and pill-box hats have given way to caps (Plate 13).

Typically, the dance begins with the dancers entering in procession in single file, weaving in and out in a snake-like figure. Then they line up facing the audience, while a 'calling-on' song is sung by one of the various strange characters who accompany the dancers, possibly the Fool, or the King, or Besom Betty, another 'man-woman'. This song begins, as do the Mummers' plays, with a call for 'room' and goes on to introduce each performer till all are marching round in a circle. After that there is much clashing and thrusting of swords, a chain of swords is formed and finally the weapons are woven together in a figure called the lock, which the leader holds high while his men dance round him (Plates 14 and 16).

The climax of the dance—the ceremonial decapitation scene—comes with the final lock (Plate 15). Here the Fool, or one of the other characters, kneels with the woven swords resting on his shoulders. At a word of command each man abruptly withdraws his sword and the Fool falls to the ground. As he lies there, apparently dead, there is a shout for 'a doctor! a ten-pound doctor'! The Doctor, usually wearing a top hat and carrying a black bag, promptly arrives and proceeds to revive the 'dead' man with the contents of a bottle which he produces from his bag (Plate 19).

There are many variations. Sometimes it is the King, or even a total stranger, who is beheaded. Sometimes it is the Fool, with his sword, or Besom Betty, with her brush, who restores the dead man to life. But only rarely is there a Sword Dance which does not have this death and resurrection drama, representing the rebirth of Nature, as an integral part. And this same theme is fundamental to the Mummers' and Plough Monday plays and their variants.

It is more than 30 years since I first saw the Mummers' play performed in my parents' home in East Derbyshire. I have seen several mumming plays since then, but it is that first performance that lives most vividly in my memory. The performers were boys of my own age, fourteen or fifteen. They were, in fact, the village boys with whom I played cricket and football. But on that particular Christmas Eve they were unrecognisable with their blackened faces and strange costumes made chiefly of coloured paper and cardboard, the disguises that prompted them to call themselves not Mummers, but Guisers.

I cannot pretend to remember every word of that first performance, which turned out to be the last in that village. Snatches of dialogue, even odd characters, from other mumming plays seen or read since then have become interwoven in my memory with the words and actions of that original performance. There are several hundred known variations of the play, handed on orally by the players and written down only by folklore enthusiasts. So my version must be considered as typical rather than as the exact record of a specific play.

(Enter the Leader)

Leader: I open the door, I enter in.
    I hope your favour we shall win.
    Whether we stand or whether we fall,
    We'll do our best to please you all.
    A room, a room, a gallant room; a room to let us in;
    Stir up the fire and make a light
    And see our noble act tonight.
    If you can't believe the words I say,
    Step in St George—and clear the way.

(Enter St George, carrying a sword)

St George: Here comes I, St George,
    That man of courage bold.
    If any man's blood run hot,
    I'm sure to make it cold.
    I slew the fearful dragon, and brought him to the slaughter,
    And by that means I won the king of Egypt's daughter.
    Where is the man that bids me stand,
    I'll cut him down with my courageous hand.

(Enter Bold Slasher, with sword)

Bold Slasher: Here comes I, Bold Slasher, that Turkish knight,
    Come from the Turkish land to fight.

My body is made of iron, my head is made of steel,
My arms and legs of beaten brass; no man can make me feel.

(*They fight, and Bold Slasher falls*)

Leader: St George, St George, what hast thou done?
Thou hast killed and slain my only son.
Is there a doctor can be found,
To cure this man of his deadly wound?

(*Enter the Doctor, with top hat and black bag*)

Doctor: Yes, there's a doctor to be found,
Can cure this man of his deadly wound.
Leader: What can you cure, doctor?
Doctor: The itch, the stitch, the palsy and the gout,
Pains within and pains without.
(*The Doctor kneels down beside the prostrate figure, and taking a large bottle from his bag suits the action to the words in the following speech*)
Doctor: A little to the eye, a little to the thigh, a little to the string bone of the heart.
Rise up, Bold Slasher, and play thy part.
(*Bold Slasher rises*)

(*Enter Beelzebub, with club and frying pan*)

Beelzebub: Here comes I, Beelzebub.
In my hand I carries a club,
Over my shoulder a frying pan.
Don't you think I'm a jolly old man?

(*Enter Little Devil Doubt, with sweeping brush*)

Little Devil Doubt: In comes I, Little Devil Doubt.
If you don't give me money,
I'll sweep you out.
Money I want and money I crave.
If you don't give me money,
I'll sweep you to the grave.

There the play ended, and after a collection and the distribution of refreshments the actors, all males, as always in the Mummers' play, went on to visit other houses. Their acting had been spirited, but the lines were delivered in flat Derbyshire accents, and it is obvious, looking back, that the players had no more idea of the significance of the play than I had at that time.

What is the significance of this play, which is performed—in different forms and often with a great deal of crude fertility symbolism—in many parts of the world? Clearly it is an extension of the Sword Dance. The dance must have come first, then the mime would be added, and finally the mime would be reinforced by spoken words. In the play, as in the Sword Dance mime, the death represents the death of winter; the resurrection symbolises the rebirth of Nature in spring.

This is a relic of pre-Classical times when primitive agricultural communities performed solemn rituals with the object of making the crops grow. These originally took the form of human sacrifice, with the priest-king, or a substitute, as the victim. Then a new priest-king would emerge. All this was to ensure that the harvest would come round again and that the beasts would thrive. Some authorities say that the revival of the victim symbolised the seed-corn being planted and then springing to new life. The leaping and clashing in the Sword Dance was to shake the earth and awaken the sleeping soil. The time of the winter solstice, when the days were shortest and Nature seemed dead, was the time to perform this rite to revive the life-bearing sun.

Not that the play is always performed in mid-winter. In Cheshire, where the players are called Soulers, or Soul-Cakers, it is acted on Hallo-ween (October 31st), or All Souls' Eve (November 1st), which coincides with the traditional beginning of winter in Western Europe. In the Calder Valley of Yorkshire it is a spring rite called locally the Pace-Egg play, the pace-egg being the Pasch or Easter egg (Plates 18 and 19). These are simply variations of the St George, or Mummers', play, introducing similar characters, though the Pace-Eggers have an additional comic performer called Toss Pot, or Tossip. Indeed the St George play characters are likely to change from place to place. In many versions the leader is Father Christmas:—

> *In comes I, old Father Christmas.*
> *Welcome or welcome not.*
> *I hope old Father Christmas*
> *Will never be forgot.*

Jack Finney is another popular character who did not appear in my Derbyshire version, any more than did Little Johnny Jack, carrying his family on his back. Bold Slasher is sometimes Beau Slasher, more often a Turkish knight or a Prince of Paradine, and even St George himself sometimes becomes King George, or Prince George. Popular figures like Nelson, or even Napoleon, sometimes turn up, and in one Sussex performance in 1957 a King of Egypt appeared looking remarkably like President Nasser.

The 'plot' of the play in this country was considered by Sir Edmund Chambers to have been derived from Johnson's *Seven Champions of Christendom*, first printed in 1596, but not all authorities accept this, pointing to earlier mumming plays. Early in the 15th century some courtiers planned a Twelfth Night mumming play ostensibly to amuse Henry IV, but in fact to provide a cover for his assassination. However, the plot was discovered in time and the performance was cancelled.

There are records of performances at Court in Tudor times, by which period the play had acquired echoes of the later miracle and mystery plays. With the arrival of the more sophisticated Renaissance drama, the St George play was banished from Court, but lived on in the villages as folk drama.

Even in villages, as part of a regular and continuous tradition, it is dying in most parts of the country. Two World Wars broke the continuity, and the arrival of wireless and television to bring more polished drama into their homes has made country folk more self-conscious about the shortcomings of their homespun plays. Sporadic attempts to revive the St George play have often failed to rekindle the old flame of enthusiasm.

But there are places where the flame burns brightly again. At Marshfield, high up on the Cotswolds, the play was revived in 1929 and has since been performed in the streets each Boxing Day morning, beginning at 11 o'clock, with King William as the hero, supported by such characters as Little Man John, Saucy Jack and Tenpenny Nit (Plate 21). The play has been performed each Christmas at Chailey, in Sussex, since its revival in 1950. South Cerney, in Gloucestershire, staged a revival in 1964, and there are regular Christmas performances at Crookham, in Hampshire, and Headington, while at Andover, thanks to an enthusiastic local dustman who learnt the words of the play from his grandfather, the traditional performances were kept up until 1963. One or two Cheshire villages still perform the Souling plays, while in the West Riding, thanks to the efforts of schools, the Pace-Egg play continues to flourish at Midgley, Mytholmroyd, Hebden Bridge and Heptonstall.

On the other hand, the East Midland Plough play is moribund, except

13. The Flamborough Sword team. This team of boys wear fishermen's jerseys of blue, but more often white tunics or shirts are worn with white trousers.

4. The Grenoside Traditional Sword team, wearing the semi-military uniform of the 19th century. The captain is holding up the 'lock' of swords.

5. The Captain is beheaded—the ceremonial climax of the sword dance, which comes with the final 'lock'.

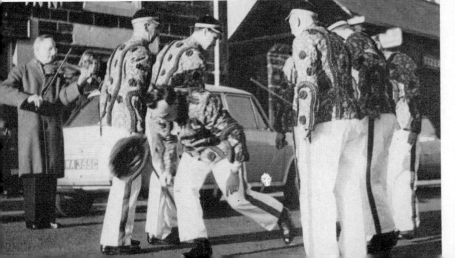

16. The Stockton Morris dancers giving a display at the North Riding Association of Youth Clubs' Carnival on Redcar Racecourse.
17. The Handsworth Sword Team of Sheffield, wearing another type of uniform.

18. The Pace-Egg Play being performed at Calder High School, Mytholmroyd, in Yorkshire.

19. (*Below*) Most sword dances have the death and resurrection drama, and here we see the 'doctor' reviving the 'dead' man.

20. (*Above*) Another scene in a Pace-Egg Play— the 'King of Egypt' sprinkles flour on 'Toss Pot's' wig.

21. Play of the mummers at Marshfield in Gloucestershire. Villagers dress up in strips of paper and parade round the streets, led by the village crier with a bell.

22. Merry-making in Tudor times at Haddon Hall (from a lithograph by Joseph Nash [1809-1878]).

23. The Royal May Day Festival at Knutsford in Cheshire. The Queen and her retinue make their way to take up their places in the arena for the crowning ceremony.

24. (*Below*) Dancing round the Maypole at Kingsteignton in south Devon. Coloured ribbons are braided and unfurled as the boys and girls dance.

25. (*Above*) One of the tallest maypoles in the country stands at Paganhill, near Stroud, Gloucestershire. Including 6ft 6in below ground, it is 94ft in height.

26. A gay scene on the village green at the May Festival at Elstow, in Bedfordshire.
27, 28. The May Queen with her attendants at Lustleigh in Devon.

29. (*Right*) Children with a 'bull' which took part in the Morris Men's procession during the May Day celebrations at Oxford.

30. (*Left*) Magdalen College Tower, Oxford. On the top of the tower at six o'clock on May Day morning the College choir sing the Latin hymn of thanksgiving, *Te Deum Patrem Collimus.*

31. May Day festivities at Offham in Kent. The braiding can be seen clearly at the top of the pole.

32. The Helston Flora—or Furry—Dance. People dancing through the decorated streets at the annual ceremony held at this little town in Cornwall.
33. Padstow Hobby Horse Fair. The hobby horse dances along the narrow, twisting streets preceded by a man dressed in white called the 'Teaser'.

for an occasional rather self-conscious revival. This play, once popular in the spacious farm-house kitchens of Nottinghamshire and Lincolnshire, was different from, and possibly older than, the St George play of the Mummers. Its theme of death and resurrection was similar, but apart from the doctor, its characters were often quite different.

The play was performed on Plough Monday, the first Monday after January 6th, Old New Year's Day, on which work was due to start after the long Christmas break. On that day gangs of youths from the farms toured the villages, dragging a plough after them. Calling themselves Plough Bullocks, Plough Jags or Plough Stots, they would stop at various points to perform a Sword Dance or a play, or both. Lights were left burning before the Plough altar in the church, and some of the takings of the gangs were devoted to the provision of these lights. After the Reformation parish records show that they were devoted to various other parochial purposes. It seems clear that here, as with the Soul players and Pace-Eggers, the Church had adopted and modified a pre-Christian rite.

Changes in the agricultural pattern have killed the Plough Monday plays. The performers who played Tom Fool, Recruiting Sergeant, Ribboner, Dame Jane, Old Hopper, Farmer's Man and the rest of the parts were mainly young men living in on the farms. With fewer young men about in the country after the first World War, the custom declined; the second World War virtually finished it. Recent enquiries have failed to reveal a single village where the play is regularly performed, though the diligent searcher after folk drama may be lucky enough to strike a revival somewhere on Plough Monday. It would be a pity if the custom became extinct because it and the closely allied Mummers' play are our only links with pre-Reformation drama.

CHAPTER THREE

May Day Customs

May Day in England is not what it used to be. Modern maidens no longer rise at dawn on May Day to go out and bathe their faces in the dew, preferring nowadays to pay good money for more widely advertised aids to beauty. We can no longer say, with Robert Herrick,

> *There's not a budding Boy or Girle, this day,*
> *But is got up and gone to bring in May.*
> *A deale of youthe, ere this is come*
> *Back and with white-thorn laden home.*
> *Some have dispatch'd their cakes and cream,*
> *Before that we have left to dreame.*

In his day it was the custom for the young men and girls to rise early 'to observe the rite of May', as Shakespeare put it, though, if Philip Stubbes is to be believed, there were some who did not go to their beds at all on May eve. According to that sour Puritan they went 'some to the woods and groves, some to the hills and mountains, some to one place and some to another, where they spend all the night in pleasant pastimes; and in the morning they return, bringing with them birch boughs and branches of trees, to deck their assemblies withal'.

Stubbes disapproved of such festivities, presided over, he considered, by 'Sathan, prince of hell'. Nor did he care much for the maypole, 'which they bring home with great veneration, as thus. They have twenty or forty yoke of oxen, every ox having a sweet nose-gay of flowers placed on the tip of his horns: and these oxen draw home this May-pole (this stinking idol rather) which is covered all over with flowers and herbs, bound about with strings from the top to the bottom, and sometimes painted with variable colours, with two or three hundred men, women and children following it with great devotion. And thus being reared up with handkerchiefs and flags streaming on the top, they straw the ground about, bind green boughs about it, set up summer halls, bowers, arbours hard by it; and then they fall to banquet and feast, to leap and dance about it, as the heathen people did at the dedication of their idols, whereof this is a perfect pattern, or rather the thing itself.'

Furthermore, Stubbes had 'heard it credibly reported (and that *viva voce*) by men of great gravitie and reputation, that of fortie, threescore, or a hundred maides going to the wood over night, there have scarcely the third part of them returned home again undefiled'.

Stubbes may have exaggerated the degree of sexual promiscuity that went on, but he was right about the pagan nature of the May Day customs. The children who dance so charmingly round the maypole in parts of England are all unknowingly perpetuating a rite which probably began in honour of the Sun God, the god of fertility.

The Romans around the end of April and the beginning of May celebrated the festival of Floralia, the goddess of flowering and blossoming plants. This was said to have started about 238 B.C. and to have been a pretty lively affair, with licentious games and excessive drinking. In 173 B.C., after heavy storms had played havoc with the vines and corn, the Senate ordered that it should be an annual celebration lasting from April 28th to May 3rd.

One of the less disreputable features of this celebration was the decorating of the houses with branches laden with fruit and flowers, but some of the teenagers took things a little far by uprooting whole trees and setting them up in front of the houses of their girl friends. The authorities reacted to this destruction by erecting tall poles, the prototypes of our maypole. Such maypoles spread across Europe, and Charlemagne, in 772, ordered the destruction of one in North Germany.

In medieval England almost every town and village had its maypole. London had several. The name of St Andrew Undershaft reminds us of the 'shaft' which stood close by the church. This particular maypole was not used again after the 'evil' May Day of 1517, when apprentices rioted against the alien merchants of the City. The maypole was pulled down in the course of the riots and was not set up again.

These riots, and the executions that followed, reduced the popularity of the May Day celebrations. Thus public opinion may not have been entirely hostile when Parliament, in April, 1644, ordered that all maypoles should be taken down.

But some may have been left up in remote places in defiance of the order; others were replaced when the ban was lifted after the Restoration, and a few have survived to this day. One stands permanently on the village green at Welford-on-Avon, in Warwickshire, painted in red spiral stripes. There is one at Temple Sowerby, in Westmorland, which the lord of the manor has to renew whenever it becomes worn, and others at Barwick in Elmet, Yorkshire, Ickwell, Bedfordshire, and Paganhill, near Stroud (Plate 25).

The Barwick in Elmet maypole, which is nearly 100 feet tall, is claimed locally to be the tallest and oldest in England. It is taken down by means of ropes and ladders on Easter Monday every three years and then re-erected in the same way on the following Whit Tuesday. While it is down it is repainted in spiral-striped red and white colours, colours that are thought to symbolise the renewal of life, and local girl guides provide new garlands of rosettes, coloured ribbons and artificial flowers on a wire foundation. The lowering and raising of the pole—two larch trees spliced together—is the responsibility of three Pole Men, who are elected trien-nially by the villagers. The raising of the maypole is the occasion for traditional May Day festivities, even though they are held on Whit Tuesday.

Many May Day celebrations have strayed from May 1st, or even from Old May Day—May 13th. An unusual feature of the Ickwell fes-tivities, usually held on the last Saturday in the month, is the presence of two Moggies—traditional characters with blackened faces and comic clothes, one armed with a besom and the other with a broom, who go round with collecting-boxes. Until the 1920s these Moggies used to accompany the Mayers on a tour of the village on May eve, distributing bushes from a cart and singing their traditional Night song. On the following morning they revisited the houses that had received the bushes, sang the Day song, and collected food, ale and money. This custom has now lapsed, and the village celebrations follow a more conventional pattern with the crowning of the May Queen on the village green and the colourful complicated dances round the 70-foot maypole.

These dances, in which coloured ribbons are braided and unfurled round the maypole by boys in smocks and girls in long dresses, may also be seen in the neighbouring village of Elstow, John Bunyan's birthplace, on the very green on which Bunyan saw a vision that 'put him in an exceeding maze', as well as at Chislehurst and Offham, in Kent, and Kingsteignton and Lustleigh, in Devon, among other places (Plates 24, 27 and 28).

This particular form of dancing has become a traditional part of May Day celebrations, but the tradition does not go back very far. Peter Opie says 'the dancing is as alien to our shores as that pest the grey squirrel, which seems to have been introduced about the same time, possibly in 1888'. Certainly half a century earlier, Washington Irving had thought that May Day was dying here, and that little would come of attempts to revive it, but he had reckoned without Ruskin, whose initiation of the 'Coronation' ceremony at Whitelands College in the 1880s re-awakened interest in the maypole, maypole dancing and May Queens.

Irving would have been astonished if he could have seen the Knutsford Royal May Day Festival, held on the Saturday nearest to May Day and still flourishing in the 1960s (Plate 23). It began in 1864, two decades ahead of the Ruskin revival, and it is now a much more ambitious affair than the colourful, but simple village green ceremonies at Ickwell and Elstow (Plate 26), costing well over £1,500 to stage. It has been permitted to use the 'Royal' prefix since 1887, when it was seen by the Prince and Princess of Wales (later King Edward VII and Queen Alexandra), who were charmed by it, as was the late Princess Royal in 1929.

The festivities open with a long procession led by the Town Crier, followed by the Marshal on horseback. Among the traditional figures who take part in the procession are Jack-in-the-Green, a man enveloped in boughs and twigs of greenery, with only his eyes visible, Robin Hood and Maid Marian with other outlaws of Sherwood, and King Canute, from whom Knutsford is believed to have taken its name. No mechanical vehicle is allowed to take part in the procession—for the organisers are anxious to avoid turning the Festival into a carnival—and among the collection of old vehicles is a sedan chair, in keeping with the fact that Knutsford was the 'Cranford' of Mrs Gaskell's novel of that name. The procession ends on Knutsford Heath, where the May Queen is crowned, and is followed by displays of folk and country dancing of all kinds.

The Festival helps to preserve a custom that goes back much further than 1864. This is the practice of 'sanding' the streets; mottoes and arabesques traced in brightly coloured sand decorate the pavements. Sanding used to be carried out before a bride's home on the wedding day. A traditional rhyme runs:

> *Then the lads and the lassies their tun dishes handling*
> *Before all the doors for a wedding were sanding.*
> *I asked Nan to wed and she answered with ease,*
> *'You may sand for my wedding whenever you please'.*

Local tradition attributes the beginning of the custom even to King Canute, who is reputed in 1017 to have crossed the small stream called the Lily at Canute's Ford after a victory over the King of Scotland. The legend says that he sat down to shake the sand out of his shoes, and while he was so engaged a wedding procession passed. The king is supposed to have sprinkled sand in front of the bridal pair, expressing the wish that they might have as large a family as there were grains of sand. The custom is certainly bound up with fertility, though the most popular motto confines itself discreetly to wishing:

> *Long may they live, happy may they be,*
> *Blessed with contentment and from misfortune free.*

If Knutsford's Royal May Day Festival is unique in size, there are still a number of villages in England where you may see much simpler ceremonies performed on May Day. At Charlton on Otmoor, in Oxfordshire, the children make small wooden crosses covered with flowers which they take to church on May Day. The present vicar has recently instituted a prize for the best two crosses, so that the custom may not die out. In the church there a clipped yew cross hangs on the rood screen throughout the year, and on May Day a garland of flowers made by the children is hung across the screen. In Northamptonshire, at Flore, near Weedon, the school-children make a floral crown which the senior boys carry on two long poles round the village before the coronation of the May Queen. Young girls at Shrewsbury have their own improvised maypole ceremony on the evening of May Day. Their maypole consists of a perambulator wheel decorated with red, white and blue crêpe paper streamers, which revolves on top of a broomstick, held by the 'Queen', who is seated on a wooden stool. The other girls dance round singing a traditional song, which rather unexpectedly finishes with a verse of *Rule Britannia*, after which a collection is taken.

A better known and more impressive ceremony takes place on the top of the 144-foot Magdalen College tower at Oxford. There, at 6 o'clock on May Day morning, the College choir sings the Latin hymn of thanksgiving, *Te Deum Patrem Collimus*, believed to have been written by Dr T. Smith, a Fellow of Magdalen, about 1660, but not used for the purpose until towards the end of the 18th century. The present ceremony may have been substituted for the performance of requiem for the soul of Henry VII, which used to be said annually at the top of the tower before the Reformation. Town and Gown turn out in force to hear the hymn and the pealing of the College bells that follows, to see the morris dancing in the High and to take an early morning row on the Cherwell. Spectators are no longer liable to be subjected to a cascade of rotten eggs and bags of flower dropped by undergraduates from the tower, as sometimes happened in the more riotous 18th century (Plate 30).

Hymns and carols used to be sung on May Day morning from the roof of Southampton's Bargate, but the custom lapsed for a time before being revived in 1957 by the choir of King Edward VI School, Southampton. The singing now takes place on the lawn beside the Bargate, as it is no longer possible to ascend easily to the roof.

CHAPTER FOUR

More May Customs

'At Helstone, a genteel populous borough town in Cornwall', wrote a correspondent to the *Gentleman's Magazine* in 1790, 'it is customary to dedicate the eighth of May to revelry (festive mirth, not loose jolity). . . . In the morning very early, some troublesome rogues go round the streets with drums, or other noisy instruments, disturbing their more sober neighbours. . . . About the middle of the day they collect together to dance hand in hand round the streets, to the sound of the fiddle playing a particular tune, which they continue to do till it is dark. This they call a Faddy. . . . It is, upon the whole, a very derisive, jovial and withal so sober, and, I believe, singular custom'.

Helston still dedicates May 8th to revelry, but the name Faddy has rather lost favour. The Victorians, in their enthusiasm for Classical origins, came up with Flora, in the mistaken belief that the celebration was a survival of the Roman Floralia. Today Furry is more commonly used. It may come from the Celtic *feur*, a fair or holiday, but is more probably from the Latin *feria*, a holy day or patronal feast. This derivation would account for the fact that Helston's May Day is a week late, for May 8th is the Feast of the Apparition of St Michael, the patron saint of Helston and of Cornwall (Plate 32).

Many legends explain the origin of the celebration and most of them mention St Michael. One of the most popular tells how St Michael won a fight for possession of Helston with the Devil, who dropped his weapon, a huge stone that had formed a barrier to the gates of Hades. This block of granite (Hell's Stone) dropped on the courtyard of the Angel Inn, and is now built into the west wall of the old coaching inn named after St Michael the Archangel.

Helston still wakes early on the day of the Furry Dance. The morning dance through streets decorated with bluebells and evergreens—it was called the Servants' Dance in less democratic days—begins at 7 a.m. and is chiefly for young people. While it is on, other youths go out to neighbouring woods to gather branches of beech and sycamore, which does seem reminiscent of the Floralia. On their return they tour the town, accompanied by such figures as Robin Hood and some of his outlaws, St George and St Michael. At intervals they stop to sing their Elizabethan folk-song, the Hal-an-Tow:—

> *Hal-an-Tow, Jolly Rumble, O,*
> *For we are up as soon as any day, O,*
> *And for to fetch the summer home,*
> *The summer and the May, O,*
> *For summer is a-come, O,*
> *And winter is a-gone, O.*

The children's dance at 10 a.m. is followed at noon by the principal dance, headed by the Mayor wearing his gold chain of office. For this dance the men wear formal morning dress with top hats and the ladies their most charming dresses. For all the dances it is the rule that the leading couple must be Helston natives, and it is considered to be a special honour to be asked to lead this one. The route for this main dance is slightly longer than for the others and it involves passing in through the front doors of houses and shops and out at the back—an intrusion which is guaranteed to bring good luck to the building and its occupants.

The last dance begins at 5 p.m. and is a free-for-all, so that this annual day of revelry, which probably originated long before St Michael's time as a pre-Christian spring festival, ends with the whole town dancing.

Another Cornish May rite with pagan roots is the Padstow Hobby Horse celebration (Plate 33). For this occasion each year the streets of the little town are decorated, and the ships in the harbour are dressed over-all. The festivities begin at midnight on April 30th. On the last stroke of the hour the Morning Song is begun outside the Golden Lion Inn:—

> *Unite and Unite, and let us all unite,*
> *For summer is a-come unto day,*
> *And whither we are going we will all unite,*
> *In the merry morning of May.*

A procession then moves round the town, singing outside each house:—

> *Arise up Mr — and joy you betide,*
> *For summer is a-come unto day,*

And bright is your bride that lies by your side,
In the merry morning of May.

Later in the morning there is a second procession, when money is demanded at each house, and the hobby horse dances along the narrow, twisting streets throughout the day.

The hobby horse is a terrifying monster. He is enveloped in a hood-shaped frame covered with black oilcloth. There is a small horse's head in front, but the creature's true head, painted in red and white stripes, is a grotesque mask with evil eyes and snapping jaws. He has a flowing horse-hair mane and tail. Occasionally he grabs at a woman in the crowd, and taking her under his gown, touches her lightly with a hand which used to be smeared with blacklead. This is said to bring the victim good luck and a husband within a year, and it is probably the relic of an ancient fertility rite.

In front of the hobby horse goes the Teaser, a man dressed in white and carrying a cardboard club, and he is also accompanied by several other oddly dressed men, as well as by a band of accordions and drums.

The most dramatic moment of the ceremony comes during the singing of the Morning Song, of which there are said to be seventeen verses, not all of them now remembered. After several verses the tempo changes and the tune becomes solemn. The dance lapses into a swaying motion, and the horse gradually sinks to the ground and lies there motionless while the song continues:—

Oh, where is St George?
Oh, where is he, O?
He's out in his long boat,
All on the salt sea, O.

After the last drawn-out 'O', there is a sharp rap on the drum, the horse leaps to his feet and the tempo of the song quickens again, bursting into the chorus:—

With the merry ring, adieu the merry spring,
For summer is a-come unto day,
How happy is the little bird that merrily doth sing,
In the merry morning of May.

Here again, surely, is the death and resurrection theme of the Sword Dance and the Mummers' play. This, along with the use of greenery for the decorations and the dancing round the maypole in the market-square, points to a pagan origin, though, as so often happens, the local people have thought up a medieval tale to account for the hobby horse custom.

According to one version, a French ship attempted to raid Padstow Harbour in 1346–47 when most of the local men were away at the siege of Calais. A hobby horse was taken to the harbour entrance and this so frightened the Frenchmen, who mistook it for the Devil, that they clapped on all sail and fled. Another version has it that a French invading force was frightened off by mistaking scarlet-clad mummers for red-coated soldiers. This story obviously derives from the small French landing on the Pembroke coast in 1797 when the red cloaks of the local women were taken for military uniforms, and the Frenchmen, drunk with looted ale, allowed themselves to be taken prisoner.

Minehead has a rather similar tradition to account for its own hobby horse that performs in the streets on the evening of April 30th and all May Day (Plate 35). The story is that a ship was sunk off the coast on May Day eve in 1722. All hands were lost, but the body of a cow was washed ashore. Its tail was cut off and used on the hobby horse to belabour passers-by who refused to pay toll.

Despite its tail and beard, this hobby horse is actually in the form of a ship some ten feet long and covered with scraps of ribbon and silk fabric. Though it has been rather lightly dismissed by folklore experts, it may have affinities with the Ship on Wheels that Tacitus described in 98 A.D. It was taken out on tour in spring to renew the fertility of the earth. Wherever it stopped people rushed to meet it, and there was much shouting and dancing. Other rather similar ships made their appearance from time to time in Western Europe in the Middle Ages and this Minehead vessel could well be a direct descendant.

Also from Western Europe comes the Hooden Horse of East Kent (Plate 34). This creature—a man covered in a sheet with only the horse's head showing—is not specifically connected with spring rites, for he is liable to turn up collecting for charity at Christmas and other times of the year in the Isle of Thanet and at Folkestone. People put coins into the horse's mouth, which immediately snaps shut. The Hooden Horse is thought to have been brought over to Kent by the Jutes, and it is possibly significant that the principal charge on the arms of Kent is a white horse.

A May Day rite that has somehow slipped into early July is observed annually at Appleton Thorn, just off the M6 motorway in Cheshire. This is the custom of Bawming the Thorn, bawming being a local dialect word for adorning or anointing. What is adorned here with festoons of flowers is a living thorn tree, the successor to one which gave the village the second word of its name. After a procession through the streets, gar-landed children decorate the tree and the railing that now protect it. The tree, or its predecessor, is reputed to have sprung from a cutting of the Holy Thorn at Glastonbury. But the custom, which was allowed to lapse in the mid-19th century because it induced rowdiness and damage to property and was not revived until 1930, seems much more likely to be a survival of ancient nature worship. (*This custom has now lapsed.*)

Nature worship must also account for the curious custom of dressing a large black poplar that stands at a cross-roads in the centre of the Shrop-shire village of Aston-on-Clun, though some local opinion clings to a tradition that it commemorates the wedding of a local heiress who was so charmed by the poplar custom that she left money for it to be perpetuated on May 29th. It is a fact that a lord of the manor, John Marston, married a Mary Carter on May 29th, 1786, but it seems more likely, as Michael Rix has pointed out (in *Folklore*, September, 1960), that the wedding was fixed to coincide with an older village celebration. The dressing, now in the hands of the local council, takes the form of hanging flags on long poles from the seven or eight major branches. The flags are left up throughout the year. But the custom is now threatened with extinction on two grounds. There is a suggestion that the tree is a traffic hazard that ought to be removed, and some councillors are reported to have doubts about the wisdom of perpetuating a pagan custom.

This last objection has also been raised by some people at Castleton, in Derbyshire, about the Garland Day custom there. The celebrations, which, like the Aston tree dressing, are held on May 29th, begin with an even-ing procession through the village streets led by 'the King', wearing, or almost enveloped in, the Garland. This is a great bell-shaped framework, over three feet high and weighing more than 60 pounds, completely covered with leaves and wild flowers. On top of the Garland is a bunch of flowers known as the Queen Posy. Behind the King comes 'the Queen', riding side-saddle. Both she and the King are dressed in Restoration period costumes. Next comes the Castleton Brass Band playing the traditional 'Garland Dance' melody, followed by schoolgirls, whose white dresses are adorned with knots of wild flowers, and then by boy scouts (Plates 37, 38 and 39).

The procession halts at each of the village's six inns, and at various other points, where the girls perform country dances. The final stopping-point is opposite the church gates. The King then rides into the church-yard, the Queen Posy is removed, and the rest of the Garland is hoisted on o one of the eight pinnacles of the tower, the other seven having already been decorated with sprays of oak. The Garland used to hang suspended from the tower for the rest of the year, but now it is taken down and stored with the dresses of the King and Queen until the following year.

It seems clear that at Castleton the commemoration of the annivers-ary of King Charles II's triumphal return to London on his birthday in 1660 has become mixed with up a much older May Day rite. The Garland Day celebrations lapsed at the time of the Civil War and were revived after the Restoration by the vicar, the Rev. Samuel Cryer, who followed the Church's well-established tradition of putting a new interpretation on an old custom. It is significant that before the revival 'the Queen' was always a man in woman's clothes.

Other customs observed on May 29th, which is Oak-apple Day, are more closely linked with Charles II. One of these is the Founder's Day parade at the Royal Hospital, Chelsea, founded by Charles II—at the instigation of Nell Gwynne, it is said—and built by Sir Christopher Wren between 1682 and 1692. On this day the equestrian statue of Charles II in the main court is covered with oak boughs to commemorate his hiding from Roundhead soldiers in the Boscobel Oak after the Battle of Worces-ter in September, 1651. The pensioners wear a sprig of oak leaves on Founder's Day and give three cheers for 'our pious Founder and the Queen' (Plate 36). There are similar celebrations on the same day by pensioners at the Lord Leycester Hospital at Warwick.

Northampton also remembers Charles II with gratitude, because when a great fire destroyed much of the town in 1675 the King gave 1,000 tons of timber from Whittlewood Forest for the rebuilding of the houses. His statue in All Saints' church is given a traditional wreath of oak leaves on May 29th.

A custom observed in Durham on that day has nothing to do with Charles II, or with belated May Day rites, and ought strictly to be held on October 17th. This commemorates the Battle of Neville's Cross, near Durham, fought on that day in 1346, when Queen Philippa, Regent of England in the absence of her husband, Edward III, who was in France, thwarted a Scottish invasion. During the battle the monks of Durham chanted masses from the Cathedral towers for the success of the English army, while the abbot promised annual masses from the same spot if divine help were offered to the Queen's forces. The Cathedral choir now ascends the west tower and sings anthems from three sides of it. The west side is omitted because a choir boy once fell from it and was killed.

CHAPTER FIVE

Well-Dressing

Work goes on very late in Tissington on the Tuesday before Ascension Day. On that evening farmers and their men desert the fields that lie round this picturesque Derbyshire limestone village to tackle work of a totally different kind in little workshops and outbuildings that stand just off the wide, grass-verged village street. Here, assisted by their wives and children, they settle down to the laborious, but rewarding task of preparing the elaborate pictures that on Ascension Day and during the following week will adorn the five wells of the village to the delight of thousands of visitors who make an annual pilgrimage to Tissington to see the well-dressing.

The work is not all done in a single evening. Preparation begins weeks beforehand when the leader of each team—for the five wells are dressed by separate teams—settles down to plan his picture and design. He will usually choose a text from the Bible and then proceed to illustrate this carefully on paper. This is the blue-print from which the dressers work (Plates 40 and 41).

Then comes the preparation of the wooden screens—sometimes approaching 20 feet high and proportionately broad—on which the picture will be assembled. These screens are normally in sections, which are dressed separately and only assembled at the well. Into the separate trays that make up the screen hundreds of nails are driven, each one protruding a quarter of an inch or more, though some places substitute a series of parallel laths for the nails. The purpose of the nails or laths is to 'key' the plastic clay that forms the base for the picture.

This clay, nearly an inch thick, is softened with water and salt, the salt keeping the clay moist to prevent it cracking in wind and sun as well as preserving the freshness of the flowers. After being kneaded and rolled, the moist clay is laid true with trowels until it is as smooth as satin.

The next stage is to transfer the outline of the picture on to the clay. The screens are placed on trestles, and the outline of the picture is pricked out from the full-size drawing. This outline is then made more clear by pressing in tiny alder cones, black knobs as they are called locally.

While this preparation has been going on, other members of the team, usually between six and a dozen, but sometimes more, will have been scouring the countryside for raw materials. These cover an astonishing variety of wild and cultivated flowers, mosses and grasses, stones— especially Derbyshire fluorspar crushed—peas, beans, maize, berries, sheep's wool; I have even seen a budgerigar's feathers in use. 'Anything natural' is the usual phrase to sum up the materials used, but the expression is sometimes very widely interpreted. The kind of materials vary from one year to the next, depending on whether the season is early or late.

By the Tuesday evening before Ascension Day most of the materials will be to hand and the outline of the picture pricked on to the clay. Then comes the co-operative dressing of the screens. This is exacting work, as I saw for myself when I was kindly permitted to 'sit in' on the dressing of Hands Well at Tissington (Plates 42, 43 and 44).

The work was done in the wheelwright's shop at the top of the village opposite the well. One by one the villagers came in, men, women and children, and set to work without fuss, each apparently knowing exactly what to do and how to do it. I asked the leader, calm and efficient in a cramped chaos of trestles and wild flowers, how he recruited his team. 'They just come', he replied simply. 'I don't have to go out with a big stick each year; people just turn up.'

Some of them had been turning up for a long time. The oldest dresser in the village was 85 and had been a dresser for over 70 years. He told me that his father and grandfather before him had helped to dress the same well. The youngest dresser proudly announced herself to be six, and she seemed to be perfectly competent at her job. Even the teenagers, helmeted and leather-jacketed and leaning negligently against their motor-bikes outside, looked on a little wistfully as though regretting that they were either too old or too young to join in without loss of face, unaware possibly that not far away at Wirksworth the Youth Club were entirely responsible for dressing one well.

Why do these well-dressers perform their self-imposed and exacting task? Why do these farmers, building workers, typists, shop-assistants and housewives tackle this additional unpaid work each year? They all seemed surprised that the question was asked. They enjoyed doing it, they said, and anyway it was a very old custom that they would hate to see pass away. Besides, had it not made Tissington famous? Visitors from all over the world came specially to see the well-dressing.

So throughout that long evening they worked away swiftly and quietly, transforming a frenzied mass of rhododendrons, forsythia, bluebells, hydrangeas, geraniums, japonica, mosses, rhubarb flowers, fluorspar and much else besides into a charming rural picture illustrating the theme of 'Let Them Glean Among Their Sheaves'.

Watching them, I began to see a definite order of dressing. Materials that would not fade went in first—such as fluorspar and tree-cones—followed by those whose fading would not spoil the picture, such as the mosses that made the ground. Finally—and these are sometimes left until Ascension Day eve, when the screens are assembled over the wells—went such brilliant effects as sparkling eyes and blazing suns.

There is an art in putting in the flower petals. Each petal must overlap the one below it so as to shed any rain that may fall on the picture. In fact, well-dressing is a definite folk-art, and one that has been brought to a very high standard by the principal dressers in Tissington and other Derbyshire villages. There are variations in style, of course, from place to place. At Barlow, for instance, the pictures always form a triptych. I have chosen to describe Tissington because it is the oldest home of well-dressing, the earliest to observe the ceremony in each season and the one I know best.

There are some fourteen villages and small towns in Derbyshire that dress their wells. I know of only two places outside the county where the custom is practised: Bisley, in Gloucestershire, and Endon, in Staffordshire. There may be others—it is never safe to be dogmatic about customs —but if there are others their practitioners keep remarkably quiet about them.

Why Derbyshire? The answer seems to lie in a geological reason. Most of the well-dressing villages belong to the limestone uplands where water quickly seeps through the porous rock and standing water is a rarity. In such country dry weather brings hardship and anxiety, and a spring or a well is something to cherish.

Well-dressing undoubtedly originated in the pre-Christian propitiation of the water-spirits. Some South American Indian tribes still decorate their springs with torn strips of coloured cotton. Such practices lingered on in Britain even after the coming of Christianity. The worship of

34. The Hooden Horse at Folkestone, Kent, is often used to collect money for charity. The 'horse' immediately snaps his mouth shut when coins are put into it.

35. The Minehead Hobby Horse parade on May Day. The 'horse' wears a fearsome mask of cardboard, gay material for the body, bright ribbons and a tail.

36. The parade of Chelsea pensioners being inspected on Founder's Day— 29th May, Oak-apple Day—at the Royal Hospital, Chelsea.

37. Garland Day at Castleton in Derbyshire. The 'King' is wearing the garland, a great bell-shaped framework completely covered with leaves and wild flowers. On the top of the garland is a bunch of flowers known as the Queen Posy.

38. The 'Queen' follows the 'King', riding side-saddle. Both the 'King' and 'Queen' are dressed in Restoration period costume.

39. Next comes the Castleton Brass Band, playing the traditional 'Garland Day' melody.

41. Derbyshire villagers
come in one by one, men,
women and children, to
begin the work of
well-dressing.

42. The decorated Hands Well at Tissington, Derbyshire. 43. Yew Tree Well, Tissington. A text from the bible is usually chosen as an illustration. 44. Another well—Hall Well—at Tissington. 45. Well-dressing at Tideswell, Derbyshire.

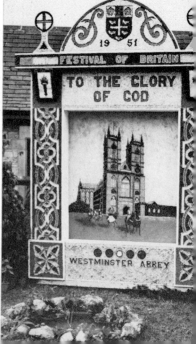

46. At Painswick church, in Gloucestershire, a 'Clipping' sermon is preached from the stone steps north of the tower.

47. The nave of St Mary Redcliffe, Bristol, is carpeted with rushes every Whit Sunday.

48. An open-air service is held in Cucklet Dell near t Derbyshire village Eyam, in commemoration of the plague, on the Sunday in August each year.

49. The procession its way to Cucklet Dell, preceded by band.

50. The ancient Rocking Ceremony, representing the presentation of the Christ Child in the Temple, is held in the parish church of St Mary, Blidworth, Nottinghamshire.

51. (Below) This shows a single garland in close-up, preserved in a glass-fronted case in the church at Trusley, Derbyshire.

52. The death of a young unmarried person with an unblemished characted is recorded in the parish church of Abbots Ann, Hampshire, by a garland made in the form of a crown decorated with paper roses and with white paper gloves hanging from it.

53. On Rogation Sunday the ancient custom of blessing the fields is carried out at Hever, in Kent.

54. At Hastings the sea is blessed.

fountains was expressly forbidden in a canon of 960, and as late as 1102 St Anselm was still condemning 'this form of idolatry'. It would not be surprising to find that such heathen practices continued to be observed in the remote Derbyshire Peak, where the Celtic blood flowed strongly even after the Roman, Saxon and Norman invasions. In one well-dressing village a native put forward a theory with some earnestness. 'They're all Celts round here', he said, waving an impassioned arm. 'They're small, dark, excitable people.' And I saw his point, for he was himself small, dark and excitable.

But it would be rash to suggest that well-dressing, even in a rudimentary fashion, has gone on in Tissington ever since pagan times. Locally there are two schools of thought about when it started, or re-started. One believes that it began after the Black Death of 1348–49, when 77 out of 100 beneficed priests in Derbyshire died, and Tissington alone escaped without a single death, thanks apparently to the purity of its springs. The other puts it as late as 1615. That year, according to the parish register at near-by Winster: 'There was no Rayne fell upon the earth from the 25th day of March to the second day of May, and then there was but one shower. Two more fell between then and the 4th day of August, so that the greatest part of the land was burnt up, both corn and hay.' Throughout this long drought the springs of Tissington continued to flow, and people came from all over the district to get water.

Both traditions could be true, the second occasion perhaps prompting a revival of a custom that had lapsed, but this is conjecture. The first authentic contemporary reference to well-dressing dates from 1758, when Nicholas Hardinge, Clerk of the House of Commons, recorded that 'At Tissington, Fitzherbert's village, we saw springs adorned with garlands; in one of these was a tablet inscribed with rhymes, composed by the schoolmaster in honour of these fountains, which, as Fitzherbert informs me are annually commemorated upon Holy Thursday, the minister with his parishioners praying and singing over them.'

A correspondent to the *Gentleman's Magazine* in 1794 wrote:— 'In the village of Tissington . . . it has been a custom, time immemorial, on every Holy Thursday, to decorate the wells with boughs of trees, garlands of tulips and other flowers, placed in various fancied devices; and after prayers for the day at the church, for the parson and singers to pray and sing psalms at the wells.'

Nobody had yet thought of decorating the wells with pictures; nor had they by 1823 when the Rev. R. R. Rawlins wrote a long account of the dressings in the same periodical. But there had been some development. Over Hall Well at Tissington, 'opposite to the house of the ancient family of Fitzherbert', who are still there today, was a square board, 'surmounted with a crown, composed of red and white daisies. The board, being covered with moss, had written upon it in red daisies: "While he blessed them He was carried up into heaven." ' The other wells all had texts and fairly complicated designs, and the first pictures cannot have been many years away.

It may have been the arrival of the pictures, coinciding with improved supplies of water, that caused the well-dressing custom to spread. Wirksworth, which had no wells, started dressing its communal taps in 1827. Youlgreave began to dress its ugly new water tank when it arrived in the village in 1829, and over the next 20 years or so other villages joined in to celebrate the arrival of piped water. In some places the custom lapsed when the first enthusiasm had worn off, only to be revived. There have been numerous revivals in the 1930s and since the war.

Nowadays you are likely to find wells dressed somewhere in Derbyshire at any time between Ascension Day and the end of August. Wirksworth dresses the places where the taps used to be on Whit Saturday and makes a carnival of the occasion with a Well-Dressing Queen and a television personality to open the proceedings. Youlgreave has its ceremony on the Saturday nearest St John the Baptist's Day (June 24th), a week after Ashford in the Water. The village pump at Stoney Middleton is dressed on the Saturday before the old August Bank Holiday, Barlow's pump is dressed on the Wednesday after St Lawrence's Day (10th August) and Eyam dresses her wells for the Wakes in the last week in August.

Everywhere the Church, which centuries ago frowned on heathen practices, has 'adopted' well-dressing, and most such celebrations open with an act of thanksgiving.

CHAPTER SIX

Religious Customs

Yet another heathen custom that has been fitted into a Christian context is the ceremony now known as Church Clipping (or Clypping). This may be a direct descendant of the old pagan festival of Lupercalia, which was the festival of youth, the feast of Lycian Pan, who guarded the flocks against wolves. Among its rites were a sacred dance round an altar and the sacrifice of goats and young dogs. The Luperci, the priests who performed the sacrifice, followed it by careering through the streets belabouring the women with thongs of goat-skin.

Today Clipping represents the love of a parish for its mother church, which is why at All Saints, Hastings, Sussex, when the ceremony was revived in 1952, it was held on Mothering Sunday, and at Wirksworth it is observed on the Sunday after September 8th, the Feast of the Nativity of the Blessed Virgin Mary. At Painswick in Gloucestershire, it takes place on the Sunday after September 19th, and at Guiseley, in Yorkshire, on the Festival of St Oswald (August 5th), the patron saint of the parish. At Burbage, near Buxton, it is held on the last Saturday in July, probably to commemorate the anniversary of the dedication of the church in 1851.

Clipping means clasping or embracing, and the parishioners embrace their church by clasping hands and walking round it in a clockwise direction, as at Wirksworth, or advancing and retreating three times while singing the traditional Clipping hymn, as the children do at Painswick. At both these places there is first a procession headed by a local band. At Painswick a Clipping sermon is preached afterwards from the stone steps north of the tower, but at Wirksworth the procession enters the church for a sermon from a visiting preacher (Plate 46).

Faint echoes from the older pagan ceremony come to us from Painswick. It is a tradition of Clipping day that the villagers eat 'puppy dog pie'. This is now a round cake with almond paste on the top and a small china dog inside, but it may be a reminder of the days when real puppies were sacrificed, just as the Clipping may represent the ancient dance round the altar. Until comparatively recently, after the Clipping the children used to dash down the street to the old vicarage shouting 'Highates', which is quite unintelligible unless you accept the theory, advanced by a former vicar of Painswick, that the word is a corruption of the Greek *aig*, a goal, and *aitis*, an object of love, and that the sudden dash represents the rush of the Luperci.

There is no need to look so far back for the origin of rush-bearing, which is still carried out in various churches, especially in the north of England. It comes from the days, dating into the 18th century, when the floors of churches and houses were covered with straw in winter and rushes, sedges and hay in summer.

In those days strewing the rushes became a ceremonial custom in which girls dressed in white with garlands of flowers and bundles of rushes adorned with ribbons and flowers walked in procession to church. There they put down their bundles and untied them, leaving them adorned with flowers, coloured paper and ribbons.

This custom, which was usually followed by dancing and games, was often observed at the patronal festival of the church, as it still is at Ambleside, Grasmere, Musgrave and Warcop, all in Westmorland. Thus Ambleside's rush-bearing ceremony falls usually on the last Saturday in July, being the Saturday nearest the Feast of St Anne (July 26th), and Grasmere's follows on the Saturday nearest St Oswald's Day.

At Ambleside the children in procession carry wooden frames covered with decorations of flowers and rushes. A stop is made in the market-square to sing the Rush-bearers' Hymn, composed by the Rev. Owen Lloyd, Wordsworth's friend who was Curate of Ambleside. Its first verse runs:—

> *Our fathers to the House of God,*
> *As yet a building rude,*
> *Bore offerings from the flowery sod,*
> *And fragrant rushes strew'd.*

The procession then moves on to a service in the parish church, which has on its west wall a mural depicting scenes from the rush-bearing ceremony, painted in 1944 as a gift to the church by Mr Gordon Ransom, who, as a student, was evacuated to Ambleside with the Royal College of Art during the second World War.

After the service the children are each given a square of gingerbread, as are the children at Grasmere, where Wordsworth often watched the ceremony: he mentioned it in the *Prelude*. There the clergy head a procession round the lovely Lakeland village. Behind them come six girls, carrying a sheet full of rushes, and villagers, with their 'rush-bearings,' made up in traditional designs. A band plays the Jemmy Dawson March, which was played by a fiddler in Wordsworth's time, and the St Oswald's Hymn is sung. The procession ends at the church, where the rushes are arranged before the special service begins. The rush-bearings are left in the church until the following Monday, when there is another procession, followed by sports.

Every rush-bearing ceremony has its local variations. At Warcop boys carry rush crosses in the procession of St Peter's Day (June 29th), while the girls wear floral crowns on wooden bases. These crosses and crowns are stacked round the altar during the service and are afterwards hung over the main door of the church until the following year. Reeds from the church meadow are taken to Barrowden church, in Rutland, on the eve of St Peter's Day—the church's patronal festival—and are left on the floor for a week. On the Sunday nearest St Peter's Day grass is brought into the church of St Peter and St Paul, Wingrave, in Buckinghamshire, and at Weston, in Huntingdonshire, the floor of St Swithin's church is strewn with straw on the Sunday nearest St Swithin's Day (July 15th).

St Mary Redcliffe, Bristol, one of the finest of English parish churches, has a rush-bearing service on Whit Sunday. On that day the nave is carpeted with rushes, and a bouquet of flowers is placed in every seat (Plate 47). The Lord Mayor of Bristol goes in procession to the church, where he is met by the Bishop of Bristol. This has been done since 1493, when a former Mayor, William Spenser, left money for three sermons to be preached before the Mayor and Commonalty annually in Pentecost week. This has now been reduced to the one sermon on Whit Sunday. Incidentally, the sword bearer, who precedes the Lord Mayor in procession, is one of the few members of the laity entitled to wear his hat in church.

A procession of a very different kind is the one that goes from the site of the old Newgate Prison, in London, to the site of the Tyburn gallows near Marble Arch on the last Sunday in April. This pilgrimage of Roman Catholic clergy and laity follows the route taken by the victims of the religious persecutions of the 16th and 17th centuries.

A similar pilgrimage is made on the last Thursday in July from

Grindleford station, in Derbyshire, to the Roman Catholic chapel at Padley, a mile or so away. It is in memory of John Fitzherbert, a local landowner, and two Roman Catholic priests, Nicholas Garlick and Robert Ludlam, who were found hiding at Padley on July 24th, 1588, and were hanged, drawn and quartered at Derby twelve days later. The tiny chapel, once the private chapel of the Fitzherberts of Padley Hall, was abandoned at the Reformation and was used as a doss-house by navvies building the near-by Totley Tunnel in the last century. It was bought by the Roman Catholic Diocese of Nottingham in 1932 and re-opened the next year after extensive restoration.

Another Derbyshire religious pilgrimage is to Alport in the wild extreme north of the county, about two miles from Ladybower Reservoir. This is for the Love Feast, which is held in a remote stone barn, now belonging to the Forestry Commission, on the first Sunday in July each year. Love feasts, with their sharing of sacramental meals, date back to early New Testament times, but the one at Alport may be the only one surviving in England. It dates back 300 years to the time when the law penalised Noncomformists. This lonely barn was a safe spot for worshippers from Derbyshire, Yorkshire, Lancashire and Cheshire to meet and hold services out of sight of the authorities. Methodists have gone on meeting there ever since.

The Love Feast is held in the afternoon after a short service in the morning. The floor of the barn is strewn with straw, and the congregation sit on planks resting on supports. The minister, who has a small table in one corner, asks for anyone who wishes to give a testimony or suggest a hymn. Then each worshipper receives a small piece of fruit cake followed by a sip of water from the loving-cup that is passed round. Each in turn then testifies what religion means to him. In this remote setting the ceremony can be profoundly moving.

Some ten miles south of Alport, a special service is held on the last Sunday in August each year at Eyam to commemorate the plague that raged through the village in 1665–66 and the act of communal abnegation that accompanied it. The plague germ was carried to Eyam in September, 1665, in a box of clothing dispatched from London to a tailor in the village, whose entire household, himself excepted, died within the month. The disease then spread through the village, killing 259 of the 350 inhabitants in thirteen months.

That the plague was confined within the boundaries of Eyam was due to the self-sacrifice of the villagers, inspired by their Rector, the Rev.

William Mompesson, assisted by his ejected predecessor, the Rev. Thomas Stanley. Mompesson drew a cordon round the village beyond which the people agreed on oath not to pass, and he arranged for food and medicine from outside to be deposited on the outskirts of the village.

To lessen the risk of infection, services were held each Sunday in the open air in a large hollow known as Cucklet Dell, and that is where the commemoration service is held on Wakes Sunday each year. Both Anglican and Nonconformist clergy go with the congregation in procession from the church, led by a band. The service includes the singing of a special Plague Hymn and an address. In 1965, the tercentenary of the outbreak of the plague, the address was given by the Archbishop of York (Plates 48 and 49).

In the adjoining county of Nottinghamshire, an interesting ceremony takes place in the parish church of St Mary, Blidworth, on the Sunday nearest the Feast of the Purification of the Blessed Virgin Mary (February 2nd). This is the ancient Rocking Ceremony, representing the presentation of the Christ Child in the Temple. It was revived at Blidworth in 1922 after a lapse of nearly four centuries (Plate 50).

The last male child to have been baptised in the parish is presented by his parents to the vicar, who places the child in a wooden cradle, decorated with flowers, in front of the altar. The child is re-dedicated in the Christian faith in a brief service during which the cradle is gently rocked about twelve times. The infant is then handed back to its parents during the singing of the *Nunc dimittis*.

Another ceremony involving children has been revived at Berden, just north of Bishop's Stortford, Boston, Bristol, Par, in Cornwall, Edwinstowe and elsewhere. This is the enthroning of a Boy Bishop, who holds office from St Nicholas Day (December 6th) to Innocents' Day (December 28th). This custom, dating back at least to the 9th century, was a serious rite. The Boy Bishop, who wore episcopal vestments and carried a crozier, took a full part in all church services except those that could be performed only by an ordained priest. He was assisted at services by other children appointed as chaplains, canons and minor clergy. During his term of office he was allowed to collect and distribute money either for charity or for the enjoyment of himself and his attendants; the lead coin of a Boy Bishop was dug up at St Neot's, Huntingdonshire, in 1958. On his last day of office a Boy Bishop preached a sermon and then went in solemn procession to bless the people.

The custom was suppressed by Henry VIII in 1542, revived in Mary I's reign and then abolished by Elizabeth I. In the modern revivals the Boy Bishop, often chosen from the choir, does not take any services.

The death of a young man or woman is recorded in an unusual way at Abbotts Ann, in Hampshire (Plate 52). If the young person was born in the parish, was unmarried and was of unblemished reputation a funeral garland is hung in church. This garland, made in the form of a crown decorated with paper roses, has white paper gloves hanging from it, possibly representing a challenge to anybody who casts doubts on the good character of the dead person. The garland, traditionally carried at the front of the funeral procession by two girls dressed in white, is laid on the coffin during the service. After the service it is hung at the west end of the church until after the following Sunday. It is then moved to another place on the church wall, where it hangs permanently, bearing on a small scutcheon the name, age and funeral date of the young person. There are many garlands round the walls at Abbotts Ann, but only one has been added in the last quarter century.

Such garlands, often called maiden's garlands because they were usually carried only at the funerals of unmarried girls, can be found hanging in other churches. One at Astley Abbotts, in Shropshire, preserves the memory of Hannah Phillips, who died on May 10th, 1707. Several Derbyshire churches have them. At Ashford in the Water four, shaped like birdcages, hang in the north aisle. In the parish church at Matlock six exceptionally well-preserved garlands, known locally as crantses, hang in a glass-fronted cupboard in the south-west porch. They are shaped like helmets, and one is completely covered with rosettes. The single garland, also preserved in a glass-fronted case, in the Georgian church at Trusley, west of Derby, has a neatly folded white glove inside a wreath of rosettes (Plate 51).

The survival of such garlands would have surprised that testy traveller the Hon. John Byng (later fifth Viscount Torrington), who as long ago as 1790 thought that their use, 'however laudable, as of tendency to virtue, will soon be laugh'd out of practice'. But Mr Byng had overlooked the conservatism of the English people.

CHAPTER SEVEN

Blessings and Beatings

When the early Christian missionaries, with tolerance, wisdom and understanding, took over and adapted many of the pagan seasonal fertility rites they ensured that much that was beautiful and interesting in rural life would be preserved, but in a more meaningful way. The ploughs that were dragged through the village streets and then dedicated to some heathen god of fertility were now taken to church and blessed, as they still are in many parishes in Sussex, Hampshire and elsewhere on Plough Monday. The blessing of the fields and allotments in some villages in Rogation Week had its counterpart in pagan times, and the litany that is sung as clergy and worshippers return to the parish church has replaced some wild heathen chant (Plate 53). The ceremony of blessing the cherry orchards every May at Newington, in Kent, might be considered too new for mention in this book were it not the echo of something very ancient.

Round the coast, where fishing is more important than farming, it is often the boats, the nets and even the water that are blessed. At North Shields, after an open-air service on the fish quay at which boats and nets are blessed, the clergy embark in a launch to bless the boats in the harbour and then sail up the Tyne, which forms the boundary between North and South Shields. At Cullercoats the clergy sail into harbour to bless the boats, and at Mudeford, near Christchurch, Hampshire, they put to sea every year to bless the water. Similar ceremonies take place annually at Hastings, St Leonards, Folkestone, Whitstable and Whitby, while at Brixham and Flamborough harvest-of-the-sea services are held each year and the churches are decorated with nets and fishing-gear (Plates 54 and 55). At Southampton the ceremony of Blessing the Waters and Shipping was revived in 1950 after a twenty-year lapse, with processions and services at the ocean dock and town quay.

At Abbotsbury, the western terminal of Chesil Bank, there are no longer any fishing boats to bless on Garland Day (May 13th). The three garlands, composed of flowers picked by children and arranged on heavy wooden frames in a traditional manner by a single local family, are now laid on the war memorial after being paraded through the village. In the old days they were placed in the bows of the fishing-boats, taken to sea and, after prayers had been offered, thrown into the water.

But there is still plenty of fishing on the Tweed, where just before midnight on February 14th each year the Vicar of Norham, Northumberland, conducts a service to bless the opening of the salmon net-fishing season. The service is conducted from the stern of a coble moored at the Pedwell Beach on the Tweed, close to Norham. Fishermen from all along the river and both sides of the border repeat the ancient Pedwell Prayer:

> Good Lord, lead us,
> Good Lord, speed us,
> From all perils protect us,
> From the darkness us direct;
> Finest nights to land our fish,
> Sound and big to fill our wish.
> God keep our nets from snag and break,
> For every man a goodly take,
> Lord grant us.

This service, doubly impressive in the darkness of a winter's night, ends just in time for the first boat to sail at midnight.

The opening of the oyster-fishing season at Colchester in September is marked by a different kind of ceremony. The Mayor, accompanied by members of the Town Council and representatives of the Fishery Board, takes passage in a fisheries vessel from Brightlingsea to make the season's first dredge. But before the first trawl is lowered the Town Clerk, in his wig and gown, reads out a proclamation of 1256, which records that the fishing rights on the River Colne 'from time beyond which memory runneth not to the contrary belonged and appertains to the Corporation of the Borough of Colchester'. The loyal toast is then drunk in gin, and pinches of gingerbread are served. The Mayor, in his robes and chain of office, then exercises his prerogative of lowering the first trawl to bring up the season's first oysters (Plate 56).

None of these aquatic customs is anything like so old as the Rogation-tide blessing of the crops and beating of bounds, which go back to early spring rites to promote the growth of newly sown crops and to protect them from harmful influences. The beatings may have begun as a way of awakening the sleeping earth.

The custom took on a Christian form in 470 at a time when the people of Western Europe were alarmed by a series of earthquakes and violent storms. Mamertus, Bishop of Vienne, then ordered litanies to be said out of doors in solemn processions on Ascension Day, or one of the three days preceding it. These litanies, called rogations, were confirmed for the whole of Gaul by the first Council of Orleans in 511 and reached England early in the 8th century. The Monday, Tuesday and Wednesday before Ascension Day were called Rogation Days, or Cross Days because of the cross carried at the head of the procession, or Gang Days because people went 'ganging' about the parish for the blessing of the crops.

Sometimes this 'ganging' became disorderly, and at the Reformation all processions on Rogation Days and Ascension Day were prohibited. However, a regulation in Queen Elizabeth I's reign permitted the parson, churchwardens and parishioners to walk in procession on Ascension Day to define and perpetuate the memory of the boundaries of the parish and at suitable places on the route to offer up prayers for good crops. The Gospel Oaks still scattered across England are reminders of some of these stopping-places.

There was obvious need for fixing the parish boundaries securely in the memory in days when maps were few and many people were illiterate. But George Herbert (1593-1632), priest and poet, outlined in *The Country Parson* four other reasons for observing Rogation ceremonies. These were:—

1. A blessing of God for the fruits of the field.
2. Justice in the preservation of bounds.
3. Charitie, in loving walking and neighbourly accompanying one another, with reconciling of differences at that time, if they be any.
4. Mercie, in relieving the poor by a liberal distribution of largess, which at that time is or ought to be used.

The custom was not universally kept in the 17th century, to judge from George Wither, who wrote in *Emblems* (1635):—

> *That every man might keep his own possessions,*
> *Our fathers used in reverent processions*
> *(With zealous prayers and praiseful cheers)*
> *To walke their parish limits once a yeare;*

And well knowne markes (which sacrilegious hands
Now cut or breake) so border'd out their lands,
That everyone distinctly knew his owne,
And many brawles, now rife, were then unknowne.

Many parishes have revived the custom in recent years, though usually without the ritual beating of small boys as an aid to memory that used to take place at various points along the boundary. Nowadays it is more often the boundary itself that is beaten, often with willow wands. At Lichfield the clergy and choir carry elm-boughs in their procession, which halts at eight points on the route to sing a psalm and hear the Gospel read. The procession then returns to the Cathedral, where the branches are laid round the font.

But beating the bounds can still be an uncomfortable business for those who do it conscientiously. At Crompton, in Lancashire, somebody must swim across a reservoir and then crawl through an outlet tunnel. Later the roof of the King's Arms at Grains Bar must be climbed over. In London the St Clement Danes procession has to take to boats to reach a boundary on the Thames, and a choirboy is let down by his heels to reach a certain mark in Temple Gardens. Beating the bounds of the Manor and Liberty of the Savoy, which now takes place biennially, involves two bumpings of a choirboy, one in Temple Gardens and the other by Cleopatra's Needle. The ceremony, which lasts about an hour, starts with a service in the Queen's Chapel of the Savoy, after which twelve boundary marks are visited by the procession, led by the Beadle and followed by the Bailiff, choirboys, jurors of the Court Leet and finally the High Steward of the Duchy of Lancaster (Plates 57-60).

At Bristol it is not the parish boundary of St Mary Redcliffe, but the underground course of a spring that is followed and beaten on an October Saturday each year. The spring, given to the church by Robert de Berkeley in 1190, now runs in a pipe whose course is marked by fourteen stones. At each stone one of the walkers is lifted and bumped against it. The pipe passes under a railway line at one point and up to the 1930s trains were stopped while the procession crossed the line, but now a detour is made (Plate 61).

Some parishes beat their bounds only once in three years. One of these is St Mary's, Leicester, where the procession passes through some private houses that span the boundary line. Another is the Tower of London, where the ceremony takes place with great pageantry, which has not hanged since at least 1555. The Yeoman Warders, wearing their state dress, are commanded by the Resident Governor of the Royal Fortress, and are accompanied by the Chaplain of the Tower, choristers in red cassocks and various Tower residents. At each of the 31 boundary marks the Chaplain cries: 'Cursed is he who removeth his neighbour's landmark'. The choristers then strike the mark with their white willow wands, receiving the command from the Chief Warder to 'Whack it, boys, whack it'!

The Rev. Francis Kilvert recorded in his delightful diary an excellent account of beating the bounds at Oxford. He was walking with a friend in Merton Gardens on Ascension Day, 1876, when 'We suddenly became aware that the peace of this paradise was being disturbed by the voices and laughter and trampling of a company of people, and immediately there came into sight a master and a bachelor of arts in caps and gowns carrying a ladder on their shoulders assisted by several men, and attended by a number of parish boys. Every member of the company bore in his hand a long white peeled willow wand with which they were noisily beating and thrashing the old City walls and the Terrace Walk.'

Kilvert and his friend followed the procession, and soon discovered that the ladder was used for scaling the city walls at points where they crossed the parish bounds. At several points 'which it was desired that the boys should keep in mind they were made to scramble for sweetmeats'. In the private garden of the President of Corpus the beaters were regaled with bread, cheese and ale, according to ancient custom, from the President's buttery.

Before they were clear of Corpus the procession was 'liberally splashed with cold water by undergraduates from the windows of the upper rooms', and at Oriel 'there was a grand uproar in the quadrangle, the men threw out to the boys old hats (which were immediately used as footballs), biscuits were also thrown out and hot coppers, and the quadrangle echoed with shouting and laughter and the whole place was filled with uproar, scramble and general licence and confusion'. In the kitchen precincts 'there was a Hogarthian scene and a laughable scrimmage with the young flat-white-capped cooks that might have furnished a picture for the Idle Apprentice'. Immediately after that Kilvert and his companion decided that they had had enough and left the procession.

CHAPTER EIGHT

Civic and Manorial Customs

In some towns beating the bounds is a civic rather than an ecclesiastical custom, springing not from religious observance, but from some ancient charter. For instance at Richmond, that gracious old Yorkshire town where the Apprentice Bell is still rung at 8 a.m. and the curfew at 8 p.m., the Corporation as lord of the manor still holds the Riding and Perambulation of the borough boundaries as they have done since Elizabeth I's charter of 1576.

The Mayor, in his robes, is attended by the Town Clerk, the Sergeant-at-mace, the borough halberdiers, the Pinder with his axe to clear a way, the Bellman and the Water-wader, whose duty is to wade to the boundary in the middle of the fast-flowing Swale. Formerly the Mayor used to take to a boat on the river, but since the boat capsized on one occasion the boundary-mark in the river has been established by wading out to it, or, if the Swale is in full spate, by throwing stones.

The reading of a proclamation is followed by a wild scramble for new pennies, specially obtained from the Royal Mint. Then the slow perambulation of fifteen miles begins. At intervals there are halts for rest and refreshments, and even for impromptu sports for the tireless young, prizes being provided by the Mayor. Altogether, quite a day!

They ride the bounds every seventh year at Lancaster, but they usually ride it nowadays in a corporation bus. At least the official party do: the Mayor and Town Clerk, the Beadle in knee breeches and silk stockings bearing the enormous mace, the councillors and aldermen, the Town Crier, the Mayor's Sergeant and the Town Sergeant with their chocolate-coloured gowns and tricorne hats. But they go at a horse's pace, keeping behind the horse-borne Pioneer, who wears a leather apron and a bandolier, in which he carries saw, axe, clippers and pincers with which to remove boundary obstacles. Bringing up the rear, on foot, comes the Flagman carrying the huge flag that bears the arms of the Duke of Lancaster. He has to cover every yard of the city bounds; ten miles on land and two and a half miles down the middle of the River Lune by boat.

The first stop is made at Beaumont Bridge, where the Mayor proclaims: 'Oyez, Oyez. This is the boundary mark of the city of Lancaster known by the name of Beamont Bridge. God save the Duke of Lancaster.' A similar proclamation is made at four other points. The records of the perambulation go back to 1774, but it has probably been held for much longer.

The Sheriff of Lichfield has to ride round the boundaries of his city every year on September 8th, the Feast of the Nativity of the Blessed Virgin Mary. He usually does the 24 miles on horseback, though a Land-Rover has been used at least once. This ceremony, which is quite distinct from the beating of the ecclesiastical bounds already described, fulfils the instructions of a charter issued by Queen Mary in 1553. After a loyal toast the party sets off about 11 a.m. and makes numerous stops for refreshment. On their return in the evening the party is met by the City sword- and mace-bearers, who ceremonially escort the Sheriff back to the Guildhall.

Berwick-upon-Tweed holds its ceremonial Riding of the Bounds every May Day (Plate 62), and the freeholders of the fishing village of Newbiggin-by-the-Sea, further down the Northumberland coast, observe a similar ceremony on the Wednesday nearest May 18th, as they have done since 1235. New freeholders have to submit to a rough initiation ceremony. They are taken to the Dunting Stone on Newbiggin Moor, lifted by the feet and shoulders by senior freeholders and 'dunted', or bumped, three times against the stone.

The thirty-mile perambulation of the boundaries of the manor of Spaunton, near Kirby Moorside, Yorkshire, has to be done on foot and takes two days. Fortunately this marathon walk, written records of which go back to the 13th century, is only undertaken when a new member of the Darley family inherits the estate, which has been theirs since soon after the Norman Conquest (Plate 63).

A boundary perambulation with a difference is undertaken by the Mayor of Rochester, Kent, who also holds the office of Admiral of the River Medway under the terms of a charter conferred by Henry VI in 1446. In his barge, usually a naval launch, the Mayor-Admiral beats his bounds by encircling the limits of his authority between Garrison Point and Hawkwood. The bounds of Poole Harbour, Dorset, are beaten every third year (the next occasion should be in 1967) when the Admiral of the Port in his barge heads a procession of boats round the harbour limits.

The Berkshire town of Hungerford has neither mayor nor corporation. Its senior citizen is called the Constable, and he is assisted, as in feudal days, by a portreeve, a bailiff and a Court of Feoffes. These and other officials are elected at a special Hocktide Court held on the second Tuesday morning after Easter, the great day of the year in Hungerford.

The proceedings open when the Town Crier, in his traditional dress, blows a horn from the balcony of the Corn Exchange. This horn, presented to the town in 1633, replaced one, still preserved, that was given to the town along with certain manorial and fishing rights by John of Gaunt in the 14th century. The horn is blown intermittently until the Bellman, or Assistant Bailiff, arrives in the streets dressed in his grey and scarlet coat with brass buttons and tall hat with gold band, ringing his bell and requesting the commoners to attend at the Court House on pain of being fined. The fine is one penny, and those who fail to pay lose their common rights for the next year.

The court then meets in the town hall to discuss the running of the manor and to elect officers for the ensuing year. Among these are two Tything or Tutti-men, who immediately go out on to the streets, each carrying his staff of office, a tall pole with a *tutti*, a West Country name for a bouquet of spring flowers—often daffodils and polyanthuses—secured to it with ribbons and with an orange at the top. With them goes an Orange Scrambler (or Scatterer) wearing an evening coat and a tall hat adorned with the tail feathers of a cock pheasant. He carries a sack bulging with oranges.

The Tutti-men have to visit the house of every commoner—and there are about 100 of them—to exact a penny from the men and a kiss from the women. Not even the coy ladies who retire to their bedrooms can escape the Tutti-men, who are always equipped with a ladder for dealing with this situation. In exchange for the kiss an orange is given from the sack. The remainder of the oranges, along with handfuls of coppers, are thrown out to be scrambled for by the children who follow the Tutti-men (Plates 64 and 65).

A civic lunch at the Three Swans Hotel, presided over by the new Constable, gives the Tutti-men a brief respite. At this meal a special punch, made from a secret recipe, is drunk. After lunch comes the ceremony of Shoeing the Colt, the 'colts' being visitors and new commoners. A blacksmith pretends to drive nails into the colt's shoes until the victim

55. The fisheries are blessed at Folkestone.

56. At the opening of the Colne Oyster Fishery the mayor exercises his prerogative of lowering the first trawl to bring up the season's first oysters.

57. Beating the Bounds at the Tower of London. Choir boys beat the 31 boundary stones with willow wands.
58. Choir boys beating the bounds at Temple steps.

59. (Right) A choir boy is 'bumped' at Cleopatra's Needle during the ceremony of beating the bounds.

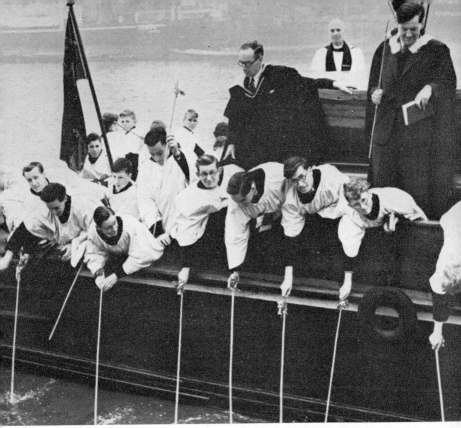

60. Beating the bounds at St Dunstan's-in-the-East. Choir boys of St Dunstan's College, Catford, strike the water with their canes on which are tied posies of sweet smelling herbs.

61. At St Mary Redcliffe, Bristol, the underground course of a spring is followed and beaten. The course is marked by 14 stones and distinguished supporters are 'bumped' on the stones during the walk.

62. Berwick-upon-Tweed holds its ceremonial Riding of the Bounds every May Day.
63. The thirty-mile perambulation of the boundaries of the manor of Spaunton, near Kirby Moorside, Yorkshire, has to be done on foot and takes two days.

64. The Hocktide Festival at Hungerford, Berkshire. Tutti men climb a ladder to kiss the girls on the top floor.

65. (*Left*) One of the Tutti men collects a kiss, in exchange for which an orange is given from the sack carried by the man wearing the top hat.
66. A new Freeman puts eleven pence into the hat after being made a Freeman of Brightlingsea, Essex.

67, 68. On 29th May each year, the villagers of Wishford Magna in Wiltshire ⟨go⟩ to Grovely Forest to collect timber. Later in the day they form a procession and march through the village.

69. The Lord Mayor of London drives from the Mansion House in the magnificently gilded state coach.

70. Before the procession of the Worshipful Company of Vintners go two wine porters to sweep the way clear with besoms.

71. Swan-Upping takes place on the river Thames on or about the last Monday in July each year. The object is to establish the ownership of the birds.

72. A city solicitor severs a faggot at the Quit Rent ceremony at the Royal Courts of Justice, in the Strand, before the Queen's Remembrancer.

73. A fine—a freshly plucked red rose—imposed on Sir Robert Knollys in 1346, is still paid annually to the Lord Mayor.

cries 'Punch', whereupon he is released on payment of a fee which goes to pay for another round of punch. Anybody who refuses to be shod is liable to pay a fine of £1.

After a further distribution of coppers and oranges from the hotel window, the Tutti-men set off again on their round. Their duties do not end until the evening, by which time they will be not only tired but also dazed by the hospitality that is offered to them at so many houses.

This gay festival at Hungerford is a survival from the days when Hock-tide and Michaelmas were the two great rent days in the year. They were celebrated with fun and games. Indeed the name Hock-tide may come from the German *hoch* (high) and *zeit* (period of time), a period of high festival. A manuscript in the Bodleian Library, Oxford, records that in April, 1450, the Bishop of Worcester ordered the almoner of the cathedral to suppress disgraceful sports and amusements in the days commonly called Hok-days. There were accounts in pre-Reformation times of women levying tolls on men for church and parish charities by binding them with ropes until they paid up. This was done on the Monday of Hock-tide, and on the following day the men bound the women. After the Reformation, when binding was banned, ropes and chains were put across the road to stop passers-by. No doubt kisses were also exchanged. The pleasant custom at Hungerford serves as a reminder of John of Gaunt's grant of certain fishing rights in the River Kennet and the free use of some land as a common.

The people of Malmesbury, Wiltshire, received an even earlier grant of land: from King Athelstan in 930. As a result each freeman is still entitled to an allotment and every capital burgess to a plot of eight to fifteen acres. Claims must be made in person each year to the Manorial Court. A turf from the common is placed on the floor in front of the Steward, and the commoner-elect, who must live within the boundaries of the town, places one shilling under it. The Steward then strikes him on the shoulder with a twig, also from the common, saying: 'Turf and twig I give to thee, the same as King Athelstan gave to me. I trust that you a true subject will be.'

Another curious manorial custom, which has gone on for more than 1,000 years, takes place before sunrise on the morning of St Martin's Day (November 11th) at Knightslow Hill, in Warwickshire, the ancient meeting-place of the Hundred of Knightlow. It is an eerie spot, a tumulus surrounded by four fir trees that are traditionally the memorials to four knights killed in battle and buried where they fell. There representatives of the 25 parishes within the Hundred meet to hear the Duke of Buccleuch's agent read the charter of assembly, after which each man puts a sum of money, varying from 1d. to 2s. 3½d., into the hollow top of a stone. This money is called Wroth Silver. If it is not paid the traditional fine is 20s. for every penny outstanding, or a white bull with a red nose and red ears. After the ceremony the representatives are given breakfast at the Dun Cow Inn at Dunchurch.

The sum of 11d. must be paid by an eligible person wishing to become a freeman of Brightlingsea, which is a limb of the Cinque Port of Sandwich and the only Cinque Port member outside Kent and Sussex (Plate 66). From the ranks of the freemen is elected, on the first Monday in December in the belfry of All Saints' church, the Deputy of the Cinque Port Liberty, an office that corresponds roughly to that of mayor. The new Deputy takes an oath of loyalty to the Mayor of Sandwich and pays a fee of 4s.

The villagers of Wishford Magna, a few miles north of Salisbury, go out at first light on the morning of May 29th to Grovely Forest to cut and bring back with them the largest branch of green timber they can carry by hand. Later a procession forms and marches through the village behind a brass band. After the band comes a man carrying a Union Jack. Behind him two men support a banner bearing in big letters the words:—'GROVELY! GROVELY! GROVELY! AND ALL GROVELY! UNITY IS STRENGTH.' The words are bordered by a design of oak leaves and acorns. After the banner march four women wearing sackcloth aprons and sun bonnets, with bundles of faggots on their heads. Next come children in fancy dress, and then men carrying boughs. When the procession is over there is a dinner at the local inn, and the rest of the day is devoted to sports and revelry (Plates 67 and 68).

Although the custom is observed on Oak-apple Day it has nothing to do with Charles II. It is said to date from 1603, when the villagers, after a dispute with the Earl of Pembroke, re-asserted their ancient rights to gather wood from the forest, but it is undoubtedly much older and may recall an age-old folk rite. In former times it was the custom to take the oak boughs to Salisbury Cathedral and lay them on the high altar while the rest of the deputation performed traditional dances in the close, but the Victorian clergy put a stop to that bit of revelry.

Another Wishford custom has gone on virtually unaltered for many centuries. That is the curious form of auction by which the grazing rights of six and a half acres of church land in the village are let for the period from Rogation Monday to August 12th. By tradition the auction takes place at 7 p.m. on Rogation Monday, but since the introduction of British Summer Time it has been altered to 8 p.m. During the five minutes before the hour one of the churchwardens strides up and down between the church porch and the gate inviting bids while the sun remains above the horizon. As soon as the sun disappears he strikes the gate with the church key, and the last bidder secures the grazing rights under what is called the Midsummer Tithe.

Candle auctions are rather more common. An acre of church land at Aldermaston, Berkshire, is let in this way every third year. The vicar, who conducts the auction, sticks a pin into a lighted candle about an inch below the burning wick. The last bidder before the melting of the candle causes the pin to fall holds the land for the three following years. A similar auction, which used to take place every fifth year at Old Bolingbroke, in Lincolnshire, is now carried out annually, as are the candle auctions at Tatworth, near Chard, and at Grimston and Diseworth, both in Leicestershire. In the Sedgemoor village of Chedzoy a candle auction is held only every 21st year: one is due in 1967. Here, as at Tatworth, no pin is used, the last bid before the candle splutters out being the successful one. At Congresbury, also in Somerset, the candle auction follows the letting of two pieces of land by the drawing of marked apples.

A very different type of auction is held each Easter at Bourne, on the edge of the Lincolnshire Fens. As soon as the first bid is made a number of boys set off to run a fixed distance, and while they are away the bidding continues. The last bid received before the first boy returns to the starting-point secures for the bidder a piece of land which was left by Richard Clay in 1770 and the rent from which provides bread for the poor of the Eastgate district.

CHAPTER NINE

Civic Splendour

Few cities are more conscious of their historic past than London and few are more zealous in preserving their ancient customs. Many of these customs are connected with the 81 Livery Companies, or trade guilds, of the City, most of which date back to the 15th century or earlier.

One of the most colourful of the customs is the meeting of Liverymen of the Guilds, the freemen of the various City Companies, at Common Hall in Guildhall on Midsummer Day (June 24th) to elect two Sheriffs and other officers of the City of London, including such unlikely personages as the Bridge Masters and Ale Conners, for the ensuing year.

The Lord Mayor and other City officers go in procession to church for a special service, carrying large posies of sweet-smelling flowers; centuries ago such flowers served as a protection against the evil smells that infested the City. After the service the procession moves on to Guild-hall, where a thousand or more Liverymen have gathered in the Great Hall. The mace and sword are placed upon the table in front of the Lord Mayor on the dais, which is strewn with herbs, after which the Common Crier calls for silence and orders unauthorised persons to leave 'on pain of imprisonment'. After the minutes of the previous Common Hall have been read, the Recorder of London proclaims the right of the meeting to select the Sheriffs and other officers.

At this stage the Lord Mayor, such Aldermen as have served as Sheriffs, and other high officers withdraw to the South Court in procession behind the City Marshal and the Sword-bearer carrying the sword. The mace is left on the dais table to signify the Lord Mayor's authority even when he is absent from the hall. The withdrawal is a symbol that the elections are 'free and unfettered'. When the procession enters the South Court the Sword of State is placed upon a bed of roses. When the elections re over the procession returns to the Great Hall, where the Recorder announces the names of the persons elected. Each of the newly elected Sheriffs becomes eligible to be Lord Mayor at some future date.

The election of the Lord Mayor takes place each year on Michaelmas Day (September 29th), again in Guildhall. Such elections have been held annually since the Charter issued by King John to the citizens of London on May 9th, 1215, a few weeks before he sealed Magna Carta at Runnymede.

The election day ceremony follows fairly closely the pattern of the election of Sheriffs. After a service in the guild church of St Lawrence Jewry, the City Corporation's official church, a procession moves to Guildhall, the floor of which is strewn with herbs. After the Aldermen have taken their seats on the raised platform, the Common Crier calls for silence and the Recorder of London explains to the Livery that they have to choose two men from among those Aldermen who have served as Sheriff, but have not already been Lord Mayor. The Lord Mayor and the Aldermen who have been Lord Mayors then withdraw with the Recorder. The mace again remains.

The Common Serjeant reads out the names of those qualified. The first name read is usually received with a unanimous shout of 'All!' The second name is greeted with shouts of 'Next Year!', and the subsequent names with 'Later!'

The Sheriffs and the Common Serjeant then go behind the mace to convey the names chosen by the Livery to the Lord Mayor. When the procession returns to Common Hall the Lord Mayor-elect walks to the left of the Lord Mayor. The Recorder announces the result, and the Lord Mayor-elect makes a speech. The Common Crier then closes the proceedings and the procession leaves the hall to the accompaniment of a fanfare of trumpets. As it reaches the porch, the bells of the City ring out. The Lord Mayor-elect, wearing a scarlet gown trimmed with black velvet and sable fur, then accompanies the Lord Mayor in the state coach to the Mansion House, which has been the official residence of London's Lord Mayors since 1753.

On the second Saturday in November the new Lord Mayor takes office. He drives from the Mansion House in procession in the magnificently gilded state chariot to the Royal Courts of Justice in the Strand, where he presents himself to the Lord Chief Justice (Plate 69). This event, the Lord Mayor's Show, is the best known and best loved of all London's civic occasions. It dates from at least 1215, when King John decreed that the new

Lord Mayor must present himself for approval to the sovereign in person or, in the sovereign's absence, to the Royal Justices. In practice this approval was soon delegated to the Justices, and for centuries the Lord Mayor has taken his oath of office before the Lord Chief Justice.

In the early centuries of the Show the Lord Mayor rode on horseback or travelled by state barge, but since 1712 he has ridden in a coach. The present state chariot, built in 1757, weighs nearly four tons and is drawn by a team of six horses who are employed during the rest of the year in the more humdrum task of hauling drays loaded with beer barrels from a City brewery. The state chariot brings up the rear of the mile-long procession, which takes about thirty minutes to pass. With the Lord Mayor in his ceremonial robes, go the City Marshal on horseback and the Lord Mayor's servants in their state liveries. The Company of Pikemen and Musketeers, drawn from the Honourable Artillery Company, helmeted, plumed and carrying long pikes, provide a guard of honour. When the ceremony at the Law Courts is over the procession returns to the Mansion House by way of the Embankment.

The processions of the various City Livery Companies provide Londoners and visitors with numerous other colourful spectacles. The Worshipful Company of Vintners, for example, proceed from their hall in Upper Thames Street to a service in the Church of St James, Garlickhithe, on the Thursday after July 4th. Before them go two wine porters in white smocks and top hats in accordance with the 700-year-old tradition of sweeping the way clear with besoms so that the Master and his Wardens and Brethren 'slip not on any foulness in our streets' (Plate 70).

Another procession goes from Skinners' Hall, in Dowgate Hill, to the Church of St Mary Aldermary, after the election of the Master of the Skinners' Company on the Feast of Corpus Christi (the second Thursday after Pentecost). Led by boys from the famous school of Christ's Hospital, among them those to whom the Company has awarded scholarships, this procession includes, in addition to the newly elected Master, the Clerk, two Beadles and members of the Court of the Company. In this procession, as in the Vintners', everyone carries a posy.

The pupils of Christ's Hospital have their own procession on St Matthew's Day (September 21st). Wearing their traditional uniform—dark blue gown with a leather belt round the waist, white linen bands and yellow stockings—300 boys and 25 girls, headed by the school band with its drum major, march to St Sepulchre's Church, Newgate, for a service and then on to the Mansion House to file past the Lord Mayor. Each boy and girl receives the gift of a newly minted silver coin from the Lord Mayor, who afterwards entertains them to tea. The Lord Mayor is *ex officio* Governor and Almoner of the School, which was founded in Newgate Street in the City of London by Edward VI in 1553 as 'a school for the fatherless children and other poor men's children'. The boys are now at Horsham and the girls at Hertford.

A different kind of procession is that of six skiffs that sets off from Southwark on or about the last Monday in July each year to establish the ownership of all new cygnets on the Thames between London Bridge and Henley. This convoy, commanded by the Queen's Swan Keeper, wearing scarlet livery, comprises two skiffs flying the Queen's standard followed by two each from the Company of Dyers and the Company of Vintners commanded by their respective Swan Masters wearing distinctive liveries —blue for the Dyers and green for the Vintners—and rowed by oarsmen in red, blue and white jerseys (Plate 71).

In the course of this voyage, which may last several days, something like 600 birds have to be examined for ownership. Cygnets whose parents have no marks on their beaks are assumed to belong to the Queen and are left unmarked. Parent birds with a nick on both sides of the beak belong to the Vintners' Company, and those with a nick on one side only to the Dyers', and their cygnets are marked to correspond. Where the parents are of mixed ownership, half the cygnets are marked with the mark of one parent and half with that of the other. If there is an odd number, the last bird is marked like its father.

This custom, known as Swan-Upping, goes back to the reign of Elizabeth I. At that time when the swan, a royal bird, could not be owned without the sovereign's permission, the Queen granted to the two Livery Companies the privilege of owning their own swans on the Thames.

An older London custom—it has been observed annually since at least 1235—takes place in the Royal Courts of Justice in the Strand on an agreed date between Michaelmas and Martinmas. This is the special court conducted by the Queen's Remembrancer at which two quit-rents are paid each year by the City Corporation for some land in Shropshire called the Moors, and for a forge which once stood on the site of Australia House in the Strand.

The City Solicitor, representing the City of London as tenant of the Moors, chops two small faggots with a billhook and hatchet and hands them to the Queen's Remembrancer, who says 'Good service' (Plate 72). Next the City Solicitor, in response to a request from the Remembrancer for the 'tenants and occupiers' of 'The Forge' to 'come forth and do your service', counts six large horseshoes and 61 nails and hands them over. The Remembrancer calls 'Good number', and the rents have been paid for another year. The horseshoes and nails have been kept for centuries in Guildhall, but the billhook and hatchet are renewed each year.

A fine imposed on Sir Robert Knollys in 1346 is still paid annually to the Lord Mayor at the Mansion House on Midsummer Day. Sir Robert's misdemeanour was that he built a small foot-bridge across Seething Lane, to connect his two houses there, without getting planning permission from the City authorities. As a penalty he was ordered to present in person one freshly plucked red rose to the Lord Mayor on Midsummer Day. Nowadays it is usually presented on an altar cushion by the churchwardens of Allhallows by the Tower (Plate 73).

The Tower of London itself is nightly the scene of perhaps the oldest military custom in the world. This is the Ceremony of the Keys, which may be seen by the general public if previous application is made in writing to the Governor. This ceremonial of locking up the Tower begins at 9.53 p.m. when the Chief Warder with a bunch of keys meets the Escort of the Keys, consisting of a sergeant and four privates, one of whom carries a lantern, at the Bloody Tower. Warder and escort proceed in turn to the West Gate, the Middle Tower and the Byward Tower, the escort presenting arms at each gate while the Chief Warder locks up.

The party then returns to the Bloody Tower, where the sentry challenges with 'Halt! Who comes there?'

The Chief Warder replies: 'The Keys.'

'Whose keys?'

'Queen Elizabeth's keys.'

'Pass, Queen Elizabeth's keys; all's well.'

The escort then passes through the archway and halts in front of the guard, which has turned out under the command of an officer. The guard comes to the 'Present arms' position and the Chief Warder, taking two paces forward, removes his hat and calls 'God preserve Queen Elizabeth'. The guard and escort reply 'Amen', and a regimental bugler sounds the Last Post precisely at 10 p.m. The Chief Warder then carries the keys to the Queen's House and delivers them to the Resident Governor (Plate 74).

At the moment when the Tower bugler is sounding his call, a liveried beadle in Ely Place, close to Holborn, will be calling 'Ten o'clock and all's well', for this is the one place in London where the watch is still preserved and the police do not go. This is the only privilege left to the inhabitants this *cul-de-sac*, which from the 13th century was a liberty of the Bishops Ely, but as late as Queen Victoria's reign the Queen's writ did not run ere. At the time when John Stow (1525-1605) was writing his *Survey of ondon* it enjoyed freedom from taxation, and was a sanctuary for iminals and debtors (Plates 75 and 76).

Stow himself is rightly remembered each year on or about April 5th, e anniversary of his death. The Lord Mayor, Sheriffs and other City ignitaries attend a service in the Church of St Andrew Undershaft, where e is buried. Afterwards the Lord Mayor places a new quill pen in the and of the stone effigy which Stow's widow erected in his memory. The d quill is presented to the London school from which comes the winner f the annual John Stow essay prize (Plate 77).

Londoners, in addition to their own numerous civic and parochial ustoms and ceremonies, can enjoy the pageantry of such state occasions as e opening of Parliament and the Trooping of the Colour. The provinces ave nothing like these to show, but many cities and towns are not without eir manifestations of civic pomp.

The Preston Guild Merchant is held only every twentieth year, but it aakes up for lost time in pageantry. The tradition dates back to a decree f 1328, and since 1562 the ceremony has been held for a week, beginning n the Monday following the Feast of the Decollation of St John the aptist (August 29th), except in 1942. The tradition was revived in 1952, o that the next occasion should be in 1972. It is a week of parades and rocessions—some by torchlight—exhibitions, banquets, concerts, ancing and other kinds of revelry.

No other town celebrates in quite this fashion, but a number cling to ncient traditions, such as the inexplicable one of weighing the Mayor of ligh Wycombe and other civic dignitaries with much ceremony at the nayoral installation in May. Many more retain their ancient civic officers. Among the most colourful of these are the town criers, many of whom ompete each August on Hastings pier for the title of Champion Town Crier of England (Plates 79–82).

A less orthodox and probably older official is the Mayor's Hornblower of Ripon, who nightly blows the city horn. This is a variation of the curfew ustom that is believed locally to have been observed since 886 (Plate 78).

Just before nine o'clock each evening a crowd gathers round the tall 18th-century obelisk in the market-place to await the arrival of the Hornblower, who wears a fawn-coloured tunic and a tricorne hat and carries a large horn. Exactly on the hour he blows a long, mournful wail on the horn and then walks round to repeat the blast at each corner of the obelisk After explaining the origin of the custom to visitors and answering their questions, he walks to the Mayor's house and gives a final blast there.

In olden times the sounding of the horn was the signal for the Wakeman (Ripon's chief citizen) and his assistants to begin their nightly patrol of the streets, a form of insurance against burglary that cost each householder a few pence a year. Though the Wakeman was granted the title of Mayor in 1604, and the police have now taken over the patrolling duties, the custom of sounding the horn has never lapsed.

The horn in use today came from an African ox and was specially made for the Corporation nearly 100 years ago. But the original horn of 886, almost certainly a charter horn presented to the city before the day of written charters of incorporation, is still preserved. It hangs from the baldric worn on official occasions by the Sergeant-at-Mace. It is now covered with velvet, and its supporting straps are adorned with silver badges representing former Wakemen and Mayors and their trades: a horseshoe represents a farrier and a stag's head a forester. Striking a modern note, there is a motor-lorry with solid tyres and a winged pair of pneumatic tyres. This civic regalia can be seen in the Georgian town hall, whose façade bears the inscription:—'Unless Ye Lord Keep Ye Cittie Ye Wakeman Waketh in Vain.' This is the city's motto, which is now shared by the city of Ripon, Wisconsin, U.S.A.

The village of Bainbridge, in Upper Wensleydale, also hears the sound of a horn at 9 p.m., not every night as at Ripon, but only from 'Hawes back-end fair to Pancake Tuesday' (September 28th to Shrove Tuesday), though three blasts are also sounded at village weddings. The horn, which is about two and a half feet long and came from the head of an African buffalo, can be heard three miles away. It was given to the village in 1864, but one of its predecessors is in the folk museum at near-by Castle Bolton. The villagers claim that the custom of sounding the horn goes back some 700 years, but a local historian has suggested that it may have begun with the Romans 'in order to summon to the camp the soldiers who might have been benighted among the tangled thickets of Wensleydale forest'. If that theory can be accepted then the Bainbridge horn is far older than any of the curfews still sounded from numerous church towers up and down the country.

CHAPTER TEN

Shrovetide Customs

The curfew is not the only traditional reason for ringing church bells on weekdays. Many places still ring the Pancake Bell on Shrove Tuesday. This practice is a survival of the pre-Reformation practice of summoning people to church on that day to confess their sins. Shrovetide gets its name from the fact that after absolution the people were shriven. In those days the festivities lasted four days: Shrove Saturday, Shrove Sunday, Collop or Shrove Monday and Shrove Tuesday. After the Reformation only Shrove Tuesday was observed, but the Pancake Bell survived as a reminder to housewives to use up their household stores of fat or butter in making pancakes, for the custom of fasting in Lent was still maintained, if less strictly than before.

In William Cowper's village of Olney, in Buckinghamshire, the Pancake Bell, rung at 11.30 and 11.45 a.m., still summons housewives to compete in the annual Pancake Race. Indeed the race is said to have its origin in the action of a local woman in 1445 who heard the shriving bell while cooking and dashed to church still holding the frying pan containing the pancake. The race has lapsed several times since then, but its future seems assured now that it has developed into a contest with the town of Liberal in Kansas, U.S.A., to see who can complete a course of 415 yards in the fastest time (Plate 84).

The rules of the Olney race are fairly strict. Competitors must be at least sixteen years old and have lived in Olney or the neighbouring village of Warrington for at least three months. Each woman must wear an apron and a hat or scarf; slacks and jeans are barred. All contestants must toss their pancakes at least three times during the race from the market-square to the church, but if a pancake is dropped it may be picked up and tossed again. The first to reach the church porch receives a kiss from the bellringer, and both winner and runner-up get prayer book gifts from the vicar.

Separate pancake races for men, women and school-children have been run at Winster, in Derbyshire, at least since 1870, but the race at Stone, near Dartford, Kent, was instituted as recently as 1964.

Much older than either of these is the annual Pancake Greaze, or tossing the pancake, at Westminster School. At 11 a.m. on Shrove Tuesday a procession led by a verger of Westminster Abbey enters the school. The school cook, in white apron, jacket and cap, tosses the pancake over the bar, sixteen feet above the ground, that separates the Lower School from the Upper School. The boy obtaining the largest portion in the scramble that follows receives a guinea, and the cook gets two guineas. Rather surprisingly in these inflationary times these awards have remained unchanged for over a century, but originally payment was only made to the competitor who produced the pancake intact. The custom of pelting the cook with books if he failed to toss the pancake over the bar was abandoned before 1860 (Plate 83).

At that time such Shrovetide 'sports' as dog-tossing and throwing at cocks were only just dying out; cock-fighting, though it had been driven underground, was still immensely popular. Children used to smash crockery in front of houses, in return for which the correct response was for householders to toss pancakes to them. If the door remained closed the children would throw sherds of crockery or stones against the door. Such customs were probably survivals of some sort of seasonal ritual for the purpose of promoting fertility and conquering the malign forces of evil at the approach of spring.

They may live on in the custom of Egg Shackling, still observed by school-children in the Sedgemoor villages of Stoke St Gregory and Shepton Beauchamp. On Shrove Tuesday the children take eggs with their names written on them to school. The eggs are placed in a sieve and shaken gently together. As they crack they are removed until only one remains. The winner in each class gets a small cash prize provided by an old legacy. The cracked eggs are not wasted; those from Stoke St Gregory are sent to the local hospital, while the Shepton Beauchamp eggs are returned to their owners for them to make pancakes (Plate 85).

The various Shrove Tuesday ball games that are still played in some places may originally have had some ritual significance. An old story, still occasionally heard in towns where free-for-all football is played in the streets, that the game began with the kicking around by Saxons of the head of a Dane is almost certainly nonsense, but some serious authorities believe that it may have begun in pre-Christian times with men dribbling the head of an animal that had been offered for sacrifice. Evidence, of course, is lacking. The earliest record of this type of football comes from Chester as late as 1533, but the game had no doubt been played by apprentices in search of what their modern successors might describe as 'a giggle' for many centuries before that.

What is certain is that after that date it was played annually at Shrovetide in at least 44 places. While towns were small the resultant yearly suspension of business could be tolerated, but before the end of the 18th century the authorities were becoming decidedly restive. Many people must have shared the opinion of a jury at a Derby inquest on a man drowned in the Derwent while taking part in the Shrovetide game in 1796 that this type of football was 'a custom which, whilst it has no better recommendation for its continuance than its antiquity, is disgraceful to humanity and civilisation, subversive of good order and government and destructive of the morals, properties and very lives of the inhabitants.'

The magistrates of Derby accepted this hint and issued a statement to the effect that if the inhabitants did not voluntarily abandon the custom they 'would execute the powers which the Law has given to us'. But another 50 years passed before the game was suppressed, and even then the military had to be called out to use force to stop it. Similar battles were fought in other towns, and in some the authorities had to admit defeat and let the custom continue.

Ashbourne, Derbyshire, was one of these. There the last attempt to stamp out Shrovetide football was made in 1891. On Shrove Tuesday police reinforcements drafted into the town prevented a crowd from gathering and kept a close watch for anyone carrying a ball. But they overlooked a respectably dressed middle-aged housewife going about her harmless shopping expedition. It did not occur to them that this Mrs Woolley, a sort of latter-day John Wilkes, might have a ball hidden under her long dress. And they were completely taken aback when she suddenly threw the ball out of a bedroom window into the market-place.

The sequel was that names were taken and subsequently fines were imposed—and paid by public subscription. It was clear that the townsfolk —even the magistrates—wanted the football to continue on Shrove Tuesday and Ash Wednesday. And so it has done ever since without any further obstruction.

The Ashbourne game has few rules. Any number of players may take part, but there is a fairly strict birth qualification. Those born north of the

Henmore, the stream that divides the town, play for the Up'ards; those born to the south are Down'ards. The goals are the mill wheels at Clifton and Sturston, three miles apart. On both days the ball is thrown up in a field near the town centre at 2 p.m. by some prominent person—it was the Duke of Windsor, then Prince of Wales, in 1928—after a civic lunch at the Green Man. Nowadays the game ends at ten unless a goal is scored just before (Plate 87).

Few goals are scored. The size of the 'pitch' and the number of players precludes that. Much of the play takes place in and around the Henmore and is nothing more than a series of rugby-like scrimmages, called 'hugs'. Various subterfuges have been adopted to open out the game and score a goal. In 1956 a player managed to get the ball into his car and to drive two miles to Clifton to score a goal. During the Second World War when men were scarce two women scored goals, and in 1965 a thirteen-year-old schoolboy became the youngest player to score a goal since records were kept. When a goal is scored the scorer is allowed to keep the ball, and a fresh one is thrown up.

The balls are made in Ashbourne by local craftsmen. They are about the size of ordinary footballs and are made of good-quality leather and stuffed tightly with fine cork dust. Another local craftsman, following a long family tradition, paints the balls white and usually embellishes them with the Union Jack and the name and perhaps the crest of the person who is to throw the ball up. The paint soon wears off during the game, but the ball is repainted afterwards.

At Atherstone, Warwickshire, the ball is filled with water to make it impossible to kick it more than a few yards at a time, and it is beribboned in red, white and blue, the colours of the local football team. The contest there is held on Shrove Tuesday only and lasts a mere two hours—between 3 and 5 p.m. Otherwise it follows much the same pattern as the Ashbourne game, with a well-known person throwing up the ball to start the scramble. But whereas at Ashbourne nobody will attempt to guess when the game was first played, at Atherstone there is a strong tradition that it originated in a contest between men of Warwickshire and Leicestershire for a bag of gold in the reign of King John (1199–1216). For many generations the match was played annually between teams from the two counties, but in this century it has become a free-for-all. Women and children often join in at the beginning of play, but usually drop out when the game warms up.

At Sedgefield, in County Durham, Shrove Tuesday football is still played through the village streets between goals 500 yards apart at opposite ends of the village, but at near-by Chester-le-Street it ceased to be played in 1930 when selected players were prosecuted under the Highways Act and it was made illegal.

A similar fate has been avoided at Alnwick, Northumberland, by the resort of transferring the game to a field known as the North Demesne. There the goals, a quarter of a mile apart, are festooned with evergreens. A committee collects the ball from Alnwick Castle and carries it to the ground, preceded by the Duke of Northumberland's piper. The game, between the parishes of St Michael's and St Paul's, is played strictly with the feet only and ends when the ball has been 'haled' three times, each hale, or goal, being announced by the sounding of a trumpet. Prizes of 10s. are awarded to the winners of the first two hales and one pound to the winner of the third, or conquering hale. Finally, the ball is thrown up and becomes the property of the person who carries it off the ground (Plate 86).

The Shrove Tuesday football at Corfe Castle, Dorset, has a totally different origin from the Alnwick-type game and follows a different form. For one thing there is no contest for possession of the ball. All that happens is that Purbeck quarrymen kick a football along the old road to Ower Quay in order to maintain an ancient right of way to what was once the harbour from which marble was shipped to Poole. By tradition this football game always follows a meeting of the court of the old-established Company of Marblers.

Further west, in Cornwall, a different kind of ball game is played through the streets of St Columb Major and St Columb Minor on Shrove Tuesday and the Saturday next but one after it. This is hurling, an ancient Cornish sport that survives only here and at St Ives. The small ball is made of light wood encased in silver and inscribed:

> Town and country, do your best,
> For in this parish I must rest.

The contest is a parochial affair between Townsmen and Countrymen.

Its object is to get the ball into goals two miles apart. Play is liable to be fierce, which explains why, as at Ashbourne and Atherstone, windows in the main street are boarded up, and why Richard Carew (1555–1620) compared the ball to 'an infernal spirit; for whosoever catcheth it fareth straightways like a madman, struggling and fighting with those about to hold him; and no sooner is the ball gone from him, but he resigneth this fury to the next receiver, and himself becometh peaceable as before'.

Although the motto of the game is 'fair play is good play', Carew was uncertain whether he should 'more commend' it 'for manhood and exercise, or condemn it for boisterousness and harm which it begetteth'. The early Methodists, more sure of themselves, tried hard to stop the game, and except at St Columb and St Ives their efforts were successful.

Even at St Ives it has been rather modified. It is no longer played in the main street, or even on the foreshore to which it migrated when authority frowned, but in a public park, and the contestants are now mainly school-children. Play takes place not on Shrove Tuesday, but on Feasten Day, the first Monday in February, the day after the Feast of St Ia, the town's patron saint. The game starts at 10.30 a.m., when the Mayor throws the ball against the wall of St Ia's Church, and finishes at noon. Whoever is in possession of the ball when the game ends receives a small prize from the Mayor in return for handing over the ball. The rest of the day is devoted to sports and a town ball (Plate 88).

74. The Tower of London is nightly the scene of possibly the oldest military custom in the world—the Ceremony of the Keys.

75. (*Right*) The Beadle of Ely Place, just off Holborn.

76. Ely Place is the one place in London where a watch is still preserved and the police do not go.

77. John Stow, 16th-century chronicler, is remembered each year on the anniversary of his death when a service is held at the Church of St Andrew Undershaft, London. After the service the Lord Mayor places a new quill pen in the hand of the stone effigy.

78. The Hornblower of Ripon, Yorkshire, who nightly blows the city horn. This is a variation of the curfew custom that is believed locally to have been observed since the year 886.

79-82. Town Criers on Parade. Here is a fine selection of criers, wearing their colourful robes and three-cornered hats. Many criers combine their 'calling' with another job.

83. Pancake Day at Westminster School. The boy obtaining the largest portion in the scramble receives a guinea.

84. The winner of the Pancake Race, held every year at Olney, Buckinghamshire, on Shrove Tuesday.

85. School children in the Sedgemoor, Somerset, village of Stoke St Gregory taking part in the annual custom of Egg Shackling.

86. This picture, taken during a game at Alnwick, shows the goal in the top right background.
87. Shrovetide football at Ashbourne in Derbyshire. 88. Boys fighting for possession of the ball in the narrow streets of St Ives, Cornwall, where the ancient custom of hurling is still observed.

89. The guides' race is one of the great events of the year in Lakeland.

90. Grasmere in Cumberland is the scene of a variety of sports held annually on the Thursday nearest to 20th August. Here we see a wrestling match in progress.

91. The cheese-rolling contest, which starts from the crest of Cooper's Hill, near Birdlip, Gloucestershire. When the starter gives the word, the competitors race down the hill in an effort to catch the cheese.

92. The Kipling Cotes Derby is the oldest flat race in England and is run over a four-mile course that passes through five parishes near Market Weighton in Yorkshire, finishing near Kipling Cotes Farm.

93. The Doggett's Coat and Badge race is rowed on the Thames between Old Swan Pier, London Bridge and the site of the White Swan Inn at Chelsea Bridge, as near 1st August as possible each year. This picture shows the Bargemaster with previous Coat and Badge winners.

94. Marbles being played at Tinsley Green, near Crawley in Sussex. This competition is said to have begun in 1600 as a contest between two rival suitors for the hand of a beautiful village maiden.

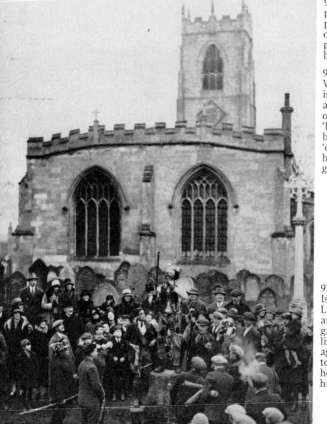

95. Knur and spell is still played in Yorkshire. The player touches the trigger of the spell with his pommel, causing the ball to be ejected from the cap.

96. The St Andrews Day Wall Game at Eton, which is played between Collegers and Oppidans. The object of the game is to score—or 'boss'—a goal by getting the ball into the other side's 'calx'. Here the umpire may be seen lying flat on the ground watching the play.

97. The Haxey Hood Game, Isle of Axholme, Lincolnshire. The Fool announces the rules of the game and advises his listeners that it is 'Hoose agen hoose, toone agen toone. If thou meets a man, hook 'im down. But don't hurt 'im.'

CHAPTER ELEVEN

Sports and Games

The people of Cornwall have another sport that is sufficiently old and distinctive to be classed as a custom. This is wrestling, and it is very different from the commercial affair that entertains television audiences on Saturday afternoons. Cornish wrestling is real and earnest. It is always held in the open air, and it provides a serious test of strength and skill.

It is a very ancient sport, going right back into Celtic history. The banner of the Cornish troops in the Hundred Years' War showed the figures of two wrestlers in a hitch. There were Cornish wrestlers in the great sporting tourney at Calais in the reign of Henry VIII. More than a century later, a bout was staged for the benefit of Charles II, who recognised that 'the Cornish are masters of the art of wrestling'.

Since then enthusiasm for the sport has waxed and waned. It was immensely popular in the early 19th century and again a century later. Two wars, despite a brief revival in the 'thirties, dampened enthusiasm, but today the sport is reviving again, and, with one or two schools adopting it officially, its future looks brighter. It is particularly flourishing in and around St Columb, St Kew, St Merryn and Perranporth.

The object of Cornish wrestling is to throw an opponent so that he lands with two hips and one shoulder, or two shoulders and one hip, squarely on the ground. The wrestlers wear strong canvas jackets, made now by a sail-maker in Truro, and have bare feet. Before and after each bout they must shake hands, and no holds or hitches are allowed below the belt. No kicking is allowed, though the rules permit 'striking with the sides of the foot'.

Wrestling is also popular in the other Celtic fringe counties of Cumberland and Westmorland, but it takes a different form. There the contestants, wearing white or pale pink singlets, with dark drawers over long

underpants, clasp hands behind each other's back. One arm must be ove
the other's shoulder and the other arm below. Each wrestler's chin res
on a shoulder of the other. From this starting position they struggle unt
one man is thrown to the ground (Plate 90).

This style of wrestling, reputedly a thousand years old, may be see
at its best at the Grasmere Sports, held annually on the Thursday neare:
August 20th. These sports were started over a century ago by John Wilso
an Edinburgh professor and editor who was a keen wrestler, aided by D
Richard Watson, Bishop of Landaff. Later encouragement was given b
the fifth Earl of Lonsdale (1857–1944), who often brought house partie
sometimes including Royalty, over from Lowther Castle.

Wrestling is by no means the only sport that may be watched a
Grasmere. The guides' race is one of the great events of the year in Lake
land. Competitors, carefully trained for the event, climb the slopes of th
steep, 1,000-feet Butter Crags, run along its rocky ridge, and then descen
through treacherous screes to the arena, where the winner is greeted b
See the Conquering Hero Comes from the band (Plate 89).

The two hound trails are rather similar to the guides' race, except tha
the distance is greater and the competitors, of course, are hounds instea
of human beings. They follow a trail of aniseed over the fells for a distanc
of just over seven miles in a little more than 30 minutes.

Another hill race, all downhill this time, is run in the Cotswolds o
Whit Monday. This is the cheese-rolling contest for boys, which start
from the flagstaff on the crest of Cooper's Hill, near Birdlip, Gloucester
shire. A specially made cheese, no longer the genuine Double Glouceste
that it once was, is rolled down the one-in-three gradient. When the starter
in ancient smock and white beaver hat, gives the word, the competitor
race down the hill in an effort to catch the cheese. The winner is allowed t
keep the cheese, as well as receiving a small cash prize (Plate 91).

He is luckier than the winner of the Kipling Cotes Derby, who receive
much less than the rider who comes in second. The Kipling Cotes Derby
it should be explained, is a horse race; the oldest flat race in England at th
most conservative estimate. It has been run on the third Thursday i
March every year since 1519 over a four-mile course that passes throug
five parishes near Market Weighton, in East Yorkshire. It starts in Sout
Dalton and finishes near Kipling Cotes Farm in the parish of Middleton

The rules cover most eventualities. 'Every rider', says one, 'that layet
hold of any of the other riders, or striketh any of them, shall win no prize.
Every rider must weigh at least ten stone on a local coal merchant's scales

But the very strictness of the rules has produced an anomaly over the prizes. Riders pay £4 to enter, and this stake money all goes to the entrant who finishes second. The winner takes the interest on stock invested in 1618, which amounts now to a little under £6. As there are usually about ten runners—except for the year when there was none and the officials had to walk a cart-horse over the course to preserve the tradition—one might expect the keenest competition to be for second place, but in fact most runners set the honour of winning above the size of the prize money (Plate 92).

A most unusual foot race has taken place at Bideford, Devon, usually in early June, for at least 50 years. The course is over the 24-arch bridge that spans the Torridge, and the object is to 'beat the clock'. The parish church clock takes a fraction under 22 seconds to strike eight, and the competitors, usually running in ordinary clothes and boots, try to cross the bridge before the striking stops.

A much older race—in fact it is the oldest rowing event in the world—is that for Doggett's Coat and Badge, which the Worshipful Company of Fishmongers organise on the Thames between Old Swan Pier, London Bridge, and the site of the White Swan Inn at Chelsea Bridge, as near August 1st as possible each year. This race, which is for six Thames watermen who have completed their apprenticeship within the previous twelve months, was founded in 1715, in honour of the accession of George I the previous year, by Thomas Doggett, an actor-manager who was joint manager of the Haymarket Theatre and of the Theatre Royal, Drury Lane. On his death in 1721, he left a sum to provide for the race, and his executors later transferred the money and the conduct of the race to the Fishmongers' Company.

As the race is always rowed against the tide, it is a great test of skill and endurance, but it is sufficiently popular nowadays to make it necessary to row off several heats in advance to reduce the entrants to the requisite six. The winner receives a scarlet (formerly orange) livery coat with silver buttons. On the left arm is a silver badge bearing the prancing white horse of the House of Hanover and the word 'Liberty' emblazoned on it. The unsuccessful competitors are given silver cups. Some previous winners, wearing their coats and badges, usually follow the race in a barge (Plate 93).

The records of the race have been meticulously kept since 1791; those of the Woodman of Arden since 1785. This body of archers has its headquarters at Meriden, in Warwickshire, which claims to be the geographical centre of England and is very close to the centre of what was once Shakespeare's Forest of Arden. The Woodmen, limited in number to 80 hold wardmotes, as their archery competitions are called, in June and July, but the big event of their year is the Grand Wardmote, held over four days in the first week of August.

Their uniform consists of green shooting hats, green coats, buff waist coats and white trousers. The silver buttons of the Society are worn on both coat and waistcoat. The Woodmen shoot with 6-foot bows of yew of the type used at Crécy and Agincourt. Their Perpetual Warden, the Earl of Aylesford, is the sixth member of his family to hold that office.

While archery as a sport has been enjoying a revival in recent years, its contemporary, tilting at the quintain, seems to have survived only at Offham, in Kent, where the quintain—a post provided with a sandbag which swings round and strikes an unskilful tilter—stands permanently on the village green.

It is curious in a country as small as England that some old games should survive in areas no bigger than a single county, or even part of county, long after they have died elsewhere, though it is sadly true that interest in these local games is now declining in some areas. Knur and spell, for instance, seems to be moribund even in Yorkshire, while fives, if it is played in Durham at all, no longer attracts the crowds of Football League proportions that it did in the 19th century, and quoits as a team game now flourishes only in the Whitby district and in East Anglia.

But bat and trap remains popular around Canterbury, where a league founded in 1922, now has four divisions. This curious summer game known to have been played by pilgrims on their way to Thomas à Becket's tomb, has affinities with both knur and spell and cricket. It is played on a grass pitch, often the back lawn of an inn, 21 yards long and 13 feet 6 inches wide. Teams consist of ten players each. The batsmen, armed with what look like table-tennis bats, try in turn to score runs by placing the solid rubber ball on a pivoted piece of wood called the trap, then knocking it up into the air and trying to hit it along the pitch between two seven-foot high white posts at the other end. If a batsmen is successful he scores an unconfirmed run. Then the bowler, from between the posts, bowls the ball underhand to try to hit a small white flap at the front of the trap. If he succeeds, the batsman is out; if he misses, the previous run is confirmed. The batsman can also be out if he misses the ball, fails to reach the posts with his stroke, sends the ball outside the posts, or is caught. A match consists of three legs (Plate 95).

Stool ball, which has been called 'the ancestor of cricket' and is also closely related to baseball and rounders, is still played in Sussex, especially by women and girls. It was once traditionally played at Easter, when, as recorded in *Poor Robin's Almanack for 1740*:

> *Much time is wasted now away,*
> *At pigeon-holes and nine-pin play,*
> *Whilst nob-nail Dick and simp'ring Frances,*
> *Trip it away in country dances;*
> *At stool-hall and at barley-break,*
> *Wherewith they harmless pastime make.*

Marbles is another traditional Sussex game. Known to the Romans, this game now seems to be losing popularity among children in many parts of the country, but it is still played seriously by adults in Sussex for a short season between Ash Wednesday and noon on Good Friday. It is particularly enjoyed at Tinsley Green, within a jet's roar of Gatwick Airport, where the British Individual Marbles championship is decided each Good Friday (Plate 94).

This competition is said to have begun in 1600 as a contest between two rival suitors for the hand of a beautiful village maiden. Teams of six now compete in a sanded circular concrete rink six feet across. Forty-nine marbles are placed in the centre of the rink and each player shoots a glass tolley—a $\frac{3}{4}$-inch marble—by flicking it with his thumb from his index finger. Any movement of the hand brings a penalty for fudging. The object is knock as many marbles as possible out of the rink, but to bring the tolley to rest inside. If a player is successful he shoots again. If he fails his tolley must remain in the rink until his turn comes round again. The winner challenges the previous year's champion for the championship of Great Britain in a match in which only thirteen marbles are placed in the rink.

A more esoteric game is the Eton Wall Game, a curiously static form of Rugby football that is played only at Eton College in a single contest that is fought out on St Andrew's Day (November 30th) between teams of Collegers and Oppidans. The Collegers are the 70 scholars who receive their education at greatly reduced fees and live in the old College. The Oppidans are the remaining 1,100 boys who live in boarding houses outside the College precincts and pay the full fees.

The object of the game is to score (or 'boss') a goal by getting the ball into the other side's 'calx'. One calx is a chalk mark on a garden wall; the other a chalk mark on a tree. Neither calx is often threatened, as a goal scored only about once in a lifetime. The play consists mainly of a series of scrimmages against a brick wall (Plate 96).

The Field Game, also peculiar to Eton, is played throughout the Michaelmas half. It is a sort of combination of the two codes of football played under complicated rules drawn up in 1847. The ball is round and may not be handled. A goal may be shot and counts three points, but another form of scoring, called a rouge, is roughly the same as a rugby try and counts two points. A rouge may be converted into a goal by forcing the ball between the goalposts in a scrimmage known as a ram.

A less complicated form of football, since it appears to have no rules, is the annual bottle-kicking contest between the neighbouring villages of Hallaton and Medbourne that takes place every Easter Monday at Hallaton in Leicestershire. It follows a hare-pie scramble that may go back to the Saxon Easter-hare rites, but is said to date from a bequest made centuries ago of a piece of land to the rector on condition that he and his successors provided annually two hare-pies, 'a sufficiency of ale' and two dozen penny loaves to be scrambled for on Easter Monday at the rising ground called Hare Pie Bank, about a quarter of a mile south of Hallaton. As hare is then out of season, mutton, veal or steak is substituted.

The proceedings open with a service in the parish church at 11.15 a.m. Afterwards the hare-pies are put into a sack, and at 2.15 the contestants and spectators gather outside the Fox Inn ready to march off behind a brass band to Hare Pie Bank, where the pies are scattered about and vigorously scrambled for.

When the scramble is over, the contestants prepare for the serious business of bottle-kicking. The first of the three bottles, which have been carried aloft at the head of the procession, is dropped three times by the Bottle Keeper. The bottles are in fact small wooden casks, two of them filled with beer and the other—traditionally the second to be dropped—a dummy. At the third drop the two teams, which may consist of any number of players, try to kick or manhandle the bottle over their own boundary, which at one point is a brook. The winning team keeps the beer. The second and third bottles are then dropped and fought for. After the final contest the contents of the last bottle are shared among the players of both teams in a ceremony at the village butter cross, the captain of the winning team being awarded the first drink (Plates 99 and 100).

This bottle-kicking custom could well be older than the hare-pie scramble. It may indeed be, as Christina Hole says, 'a survival of the

ymbolic driving away of winter which often formed part of rural spring
estivals'. It is certainly deeply entrenched in the hearts of Hallaton people,
s an 18th-century rector discovered when he proposed to drop the cus-
om and use the pies-and-ale money for some worthier cause. He found
he words 'No pie, no parson and a job for the glazier' chalked all over the
ectory walls, and wisely changed his plans.

If the symbolic struggle between winter and spring is represented at
Hallaton, it is even more clearly evident in the Haxey Hood game. There
s more than a hint here of animal—perhaps even of human—sacrifice.

In the Isle of Axholme, however, tradition plants the start of the
custom firmly in the 13th century. The belief is that a Lady Mowbray,
wife of a powerful landowner in this part of North Lincolnshire, lost her
hood when riding to church. Twelve labourers retrieved it, and she was
so impressed by this piece of courtesy that she gave to the village of Haxey
a piece of land, still called the Hoodland, the rent from which should pay
for a hood that was to be contested for annually by twelve villagers dressed
in scarlet jerkins and caps.

The game as it is played today suggests something straight out of
Michael Bentine's *Square World*, but it is taken so seriously that prepara-
tions begin as early as St John's Eve (June 23rd) when a King Boggon and
a committee of twelve are elected. The game is played on Plough Monday.

That day is a holiday in the village from noon. The fun starts at 2 p.m.
on the Church Green to the pealing of the church bells, welcoming the
arrival of the King Boggon and his attendants. The King Boggon carries
his wand of office of thirteen willow wands bound with thirteen bands of
willow and wears ceremonial dress, including a tall hat decorated with
red flowers. With him are twelve Boggons, also with tall hats and wearing
pink jackets, and a Fool with blackened face and grotesque costume with
paper streamers hanging down his back.

The Fool mounts the stone base of what was once the village cross and
recounts the story of the origin of the event in a rambling speech that
follows a traditional form. He then announces the rules of the game and
advises his listeners that it is 'Hoose agen hoose, toone agen toone. If
thou meets a man, hook 'im down. But don't 'urt 'im'.

While he is speaking his streamers are set alight and a match is put to
some dampened straw at his feet. This rite, with its suggestion of human
sacrifice, is called Smoking the Fool.

When the fire has been put out, the Boggons lead the way up to the top
of Haxey Hill. There, at a point on the boundary line between Haxey and

Westwoodside, the Boggons surround their King at a distance of about 100 yards. The King Boggon throws up the first 'hood', a tightly bound roll of sacking. The person securing it tries to elude the ring and carry his prize to the nearest pub, to be rewarded with one shilling. But if he is tackled by a Boggon, the hood is returned to the King to be thrown up again.

After the first twelve hoods have been disposed of in this way, the game changes character. The thirteenth hood, made of leather, is thrown up, and the 'Sway' begins. Rival teams, sometimes hundreds strong, try to force the hood into one of the three local inns. A vast rugby scrum heaves its way downhill, sweeping aside anything in its path. Then there are free drinks all round, and the winning pub keeps the hood until Haxey Day comes round again (Plate 97).

It is all good fun, but behind it lies something old and dark and rather sinister. E. O. James, noting a reference in the Fool's speech to half a bullock running about a field, thinks that the hood represents the half-head of a bull sacrificed to fertilise newly ploughed fields, and therefore eagerly sought by those wanting to use it on their own crops. And what of Smoking the Fool? Was it an act of ritual fumigation, the last rite at the end of a midwinter festival? If so, where did it end?

CHAPTER TWELVE

Doles and Charities

After this almost frightening excursion into pagan Britain it is something of a relief to turn to a custom that is wholly Christian in origin. This is the distribution of the Royal Maundy that takes place each year on Maundy Thursday, the day before Good Friday. It commemorates Christ's washing of the feet of His disciples at the Last Supper. The word Maundy is derived from the Latin *mandatum*, through Old French *maundé*, an order or command.

The observance of this custom has been traced back to the 4th century, and a 6th-century account shows that it was then being carried out by St Brendan and his monks. Two centuries later the poet and theologian Alcuin described the form of the Maundy celebration in his *Book of Offices*. The custom of that time in the monasteries was for the monks to wash the feet of as many poor people as there were monks in that particular religious community.

There is a record that Edward I (1272–1307) gave money on Easter Eve to thirteen poor people whose feet the Queen had washed, but his successor, Edward II (1307–27), may have been the first sovereign to wash the feet of the poor himself. Edward III (1327–77) seems to have introduced the practice of distributing gifts equal in number to the years of the sovereign's age.

In those days food and clothes, as well as money, were given to the poor. Queen Mary in 1556 gave the robe she had worn at a celebration to the oldest and poorest woman present. Queen Elizabeth I in 1572, when she was 39, gave to each of the 39 poor women 'certain yardes of broad clothe to make a gowne and a pair of sleeves'. Afterwards she presented each with a wooden dish on which was a large piece of salmon, as much ling, six red herrings and loaves of cheat bread (good wheaten bread), all of which was washed down with claret. This followed a long, elaborate ceremony in which the women had their feet washed in turn by the 'laundresse', the sub-almoner and the almoner, and finally by the Queen herself, who 'kneeling down upon the cushion, in succession washed one foot of every one of the 39 women, in so many silver basins, containing warm water and sweet scented flowers . . .'.

James II is usually credited with being the last sovereign to perform the feet-washing ceremony, but there is a record that William III 'came to the Banqueting House from Kensington and washed the feet of 12 poor men and gave them money and cloth to make them garments'. By then, however, the washing operation had been simplified; it was done by sprinkling the feet with a sprig of hyssop dipped in water. It gradually came to be delegated to the Lord High Almoner, the Archbishop of Canterbury, and by the mid-18th century it was discontinued.

The four Georges gave alms liberally, though by proxy, together with generous helpings of boiled beef and shoulder of mutton, but by Queen Victoria's time the feast had been dropped. She for a time continued to give clothing, mostly woollens, but afterwards substituted a purse of money, since when money only has been distributed.

The present Queen, like her immediate predecessors, makes a point of attending the Maundy ceremony and distributing the Maundy Money herself. Since 1953, when Westminster Abbey was being prepared for the Coronation, the practice has sprung up of holding the Maundy service and distribution in other cathedrals.

The Queen and clergy carry posies, the traditional protection against fever and plague. During the ceremony the clergy remove their vestments and are clad only in white, with a linen towel on the shoulder to commemorate the custom of washing the feet (Plate 101).

The money is in small leather purses, some red, some white, with long strings—the purse strings such as successive Chancellors of the Exchequer exhort us to tighten—carried on a large gold alms-dish by a Yeoman of the Guard. The red purses contain the money given in place of food and clothing. In the white purses is the Maundy Money. This consists of specially minted silver coins to the value of one penny, twopence, three-pence and fourpence of the same size as those minted in the reign of Charles II. The amount given is at the rate of one penny for each year of the sovereign's age. Thus in 1965 the 39 men and 39 women chosen from the diocese of Canterbury received coins to the value of 39 pence at the ceremony in Canterbury Cathedral. These coins are, by special dispensation, legal tender, but most recipients are proud to keep them, although *The Observer* reported on April 18th, 1965, that some dealers were prepared to offer as much as £75 for a white purse containing a set of 39 coins (Plate 102).

Another ceremony which the sovereign attends either in person or by proxy is the Royal Epiphany service in the Chapel Royal, St James's, on the Feast of the Epiphany (January 6th). It commemorates the gifts of the Magi and can be traced back to at least 1730. Sovereigns used to attend in person, but ever since the Regency it has been more usual for the monarch to be represented by the Lord Chamberlain. Wearing his robes and attended by Yeomen of the Guard, he presents three purses, representing the gifts of gold, frankincense and myrrh, while the offertory is being read. The purses now contain money, which is distributed afterwards among the poor of the parish.

Many gifts of cash or goods to the poor, such as Ralph Greneway's at Wiveton, originated long before the first Elizabethan Poor Law signposted the way to the Welfare State. One of the oldest is the famous Tichborne Dole, under the terms of which the men, women and children of Tichborne and the adjoining Hampshire village of Cheriton receive between them 30 hundredweight of flour each year.

An interesting story explains the origin of this Dole. Way back in the 12th century, Lady Mabella Tichborne, on her death-bed begged her husband to let her establish a dole of bread for all who came to Tichborne on the Feast of the Annunciation (March 25th). Sir Roger, less inclined to good works, snatched a brand from the fire and promised his wife to allocate flour from the produce of as much land as she could encircle while it continued to burn. She insisted on being carried to a spot near the house and, summoning her last reserves of energy, managed to crawl round $23\frac{1}{2}$ acres of land before the brand burnt out. This land, known to this day as the Crawls, still produces the annual dole of flour.

Just before she died Lady Mabella prophesied that should the Dole ever be discontinued a generation of seven sons would be followed by a generation of seven daughters and the family would die out. In the late 18th century, Sir Henry Tichborne, alarmed at the disorderly rabble that attended the Dole, substituted a gift of money to the church for the then customary gift of small loaves, a generation of seven sons was followed by one of seven daughters, and the Dole was resumed.

As the Tichborne family are Roman Catholics, the distribution follows a short service in Latin, at which prayers are offered for the founder's soul.

The flour is issued from an enormous bin on the steps of Tichborne House by the head of the family and his heir. Every male adult receives one gallon of flour and the women and children half a gallon each. When Sir Anthony Tichborne failed to get extra bread units from the Ministry of Food in 1947 at a time when bread was still rationed, he received 6,000 coupons for flour from well-wishers all over the country (Plate 103).

In Berkshire, the Ufton Dole is still distributed to the 'poore of Ufton' from a hall window of Ufton Court on a movable date 'about the middle of Lent', as it has been since the reign of the first Elizabeth. Under the terms of the will of Lady Elizabeth Marvin, who died in 1581, the dole took the form of 164 loaves, 12½ ells of canvas and 12½ yards of calico or flannel, but in modern times this has been freely interpreted as gifts of bread and linen or clothing (Plate 104).

A more widely publicised charity is the Biddenden Dole. This is instituted under the terms of the will of the Biddenden maids, Eliza and Mary Chaulkhurst. They were Siamese twins, joined together at hip and shoulder, who were reputedly born in the year 1100, though a date some four centuries later seems more likely. They died within six hours of each other at the age of 34 and left twenty acres of land to the churchwardens to provide bread and cheese for the needy of their Kentish parish. In 1636 the then rector tried to add the land to his glebe, but the court that heard his case ruled that the property belonged to the parish for the use of its poor. Six acres of what is still called the Bread and Cheese Land were sold some years ago and the area is now occupied by Council cottages forming the Chaulkhurst estate. This sale greatly increased the income of the charity.

The Dole is now distributed in the form of two four-pound loaves and one pound of cheese on Easter Sunday from the window of one of the old workhouse cottages that stand on land left by the twins. In addition Biddenden cakes, hard biscuits bearing the impress of the joined sisters and the date 1100, are issued to all who apply for them (Plate 105).

Bread and cheese has to be scrambled for at St Briavels, in the Forest of Dean, every Whit Sunday evening. Men standing on a ten-foot high wall by the church throw the food from baskets to the congregation leaving after evensong. The origin of the custom is obscure, but a picturesque local tradition has it that it commemorates the rights granted by King John to the villagers to graze their animals and gather wood from 1,000 acres of land called the Hudnalls, a privilege obtained for them by a courageous Countess of Hereford who emulated Lady Godiva by riding aked through the village. The villagers, with a spirit worthy of their egendary patroness, maintained their custom through the war years by acrificing some of their cheese rations.

Bread alone is served to poor and aged folk in the Somerset parish of Keynsham at Christmas time, as it has been since the institution in 1619 of he Holbin Charity, one of the numerous Christmas doles that are still distributed up and down the country.

Buns are issued to 500 children after a special service at St Michael's Church, Bristol, on Easter Tuesday. The origin of this custom dates back o the days when poor people could afford only black bread, and this pecial occasion offered them at least one meal of white bread a year. The buns, which have replaced the bread in recent years, are known as 2d. tarvers (Plate 106).

Similarly, cakes and ale are no longer served to the people of Hentland, Sellack and King's Capel, all near Ross-on-Wye, in Herefordshire, on Palm Sunday. Instead each parishioner, on leaving the church after service on that day, receives from the vicar a small individual cake called a Pax Cake, bearing the impress of the Paschal Lamb. The original purpose of the cakes and ale, provided under the terms of a 16th-century will made by a Lady Scudamore, and consumed in church, was to promote by means of a communal meal the spirit of peace and good fellowship before the Easter Sunday Communion. This explains the greeting, 'God and Good Neighbourhood' that is still given with the Pax Cakes.

A similar idea lies behind the annual Peace and Good Neighbourhood dinner at Kidderminster. More than 500 years ago a small legacy was left to provide money for the gift of loaves to children born or living in Church Street and for an annual meeting of the men of Church Street to settle any differences that might have arisen among them. A further legacy 200 years ago provided for gifts, including ale and tobacco, for the men. A local committee now administers the charity and holds the feast at which the toast 'Peace and Good Neighbourhood' is honoured.

A horn of ale and a small square of bread are still given to any traveller who asks for the Wayfarer's Dole at the gatehouse of the Hospital of St Cross in Winchester, as it has been since the almshouse was founded by Henry de Blois, Bishop of Winchester, in 1136 (Plate 108). This dole is unusual in being available for the asking.

Many benefactors imposed conditions that were often directed towards ensuring that their own names were not forgotten. A Robert Rede, of Burnham, for instance, who died in 1514, left instructions in his will that

every February 27th 'while the world shall endure' twopence should b
given to every Colleger in Hall at Eton College who would recall hi
memory and that of his wife at the altar. Provost Roger Lupton, who die
in 1535, raised the sum to threepence.

John Knill, an 18th-century collector of customs at St Ives, in Cornwal
and a former mayor of the town, went even further in his determination t
perpetuate his name. In addition to building himself a 50-foot-high granit
mausoleum—which in fact he never used—on Worvas Hill, just outsid
St Ives, he directed that on St James's Day (July 25th) every five years te
little girls not more than ten years old should dance to the tunes of a fiddl
for fifteen minutes round his monument while singing the Old Hundredth
psalm. The children were to receive £5 between them and the fiddler £1
Two widows aged at least 64 who went with the children were to b
given £2 each, and various other bequests were made. This quinquennia
ceremony (next due in 1971) has become a festive occasion, with th
mayor leading the procession to Knill's Needle and a civic dinner later ir
the day.

There are several charities where the recipients have to take money
from the donor's tombstone, or even to walk over the tomb. At S
Bartholomew's the Great, Smithfield, 21 sixpences are given to 21 poor
widows every Good Friday under the terms of the Butterworth Charity
of 1686. The coins are placed on a tombstone in the churchyard and each
widow kneels by the stone to pick up her sixpence. She then walks over
the stone and is given a hot cross bun and half a crown (Plate 109).

At Eldersfield, in Worcestershire, 'the honest poor, not Bastards nor
any known dishonest poor' who benefit from the will made by William
Underhill in 1647, are spared on account of age from kneeling to pick up
their alms from their benefactor's tomb on the floor of the aisle of the
parish church. Instead they are now handed the money by a churchwarden,
who sits on a chair at the head of the tomb while the vicar calls the names
of the beneficiaries. The money is distributed on the Sundays nearest to
St Thomas's Day (December 21st) and St John the Baptist's Day (January
7th) after morning service.

The five poor boys under sixteen who qualify for 40 shillings each
under the terms of a will left by William Glanville, a Treasury clerk, in
1717, have to recite the Lord's Prayer, the Apostle's Creed and the Ten
Commandments while standing with their right hands resting on the
tomb of the donor in Wotton churchyard, near Dorking, Surrey. The
boys also have to read aloud the fifteenth chapter of the First Epistle of St

Paul to the Corinthians and write two verses of the Epistle in clear and legible writing. The annual test is supposed to take place early in February, but it is sometimes postponed to a date nearer Ascension Day in the hope of better weather. Even so, it is frequently necessary to enclose the tomb in a tent for the occasion.

A throw of the dice decides the recipient of John How's Charity at Guildford. At his death in 1674 John How left instructions that the interest on £400 should be diced for at the end of January each year between two maidservants, who must not be employed in beer houses or hostelries, the winner taking all. But the runner-up now gets the interest on money left by John Parsons in 1702 and originally intended for a 'poor young man' who had served a seven-year apprenticeship in Guildford. As Parsons left £600, it follows that, as in the case of the Kipling Cotes Derby, the runner-up gains most (Plate 107).

Dicing, directed by the vicar, also decides who shall win six Bibles each Whit Monday at St Ives, Huntingdonshire. Twelve children, six Church of England and six Nonconformist, throw the dice in accordance with the terms of the will left by Dr Robert Wilde in 1675, the money for the Bibles coming originally from the rent of a piece of land known as Bible Orchard. The land was later sold and the money invested. The dicing took place on the altar of the parish church until 1880, when it was transferred to a table near the chancel steps. Since 1918 it has been held in the nearby church school.

CHAPTER THIRTEEN

Ancient Courts

In most years, immediately after Whit Monday, some newspaper or other comes up with an amusing little story about the trial for the Dunmow Flitch. The mock court with its jury of six bachelors and six spinsters that now sits annually at either Great Dunmow, Saffron Walden or Ilford takes part in a gay little frolic, a dramatised version of the old joke about the horrors of matrimony. But it is also preserving a custom that may have started more than 700 years ago.

A folk rhyme of unknown date records:—

He that repents not of his marriage in a year and a day either sleeping or waking
May lawfully go to Dunmow and fetch him a gammon of bacon.

But nobody is certain when this was first possible. The earliest known winner—his name is recorded in the cartulary of Little Dunmow Priory— was Robert Wright, of Badbury, in 1445. Yet there certainly were earlier claimants. Langland, in the 14th century, mentioned the flitch. Chaucer's Wife of Bath said of three of her husbands (in Nevill Coghill's translation):—

Never for them the flitch of bacon though
That some have won in Essex at Dunmow.

And this was more than half a century before Wright's success.

The local tradition that ascribes the foundation of the custom to Robert FitzWalter around 1246 may well be right, but the basic idea possibly came from the Abbey of St Melaine, in Brittany, where a similar custom was observed. Perhaps originally the distribution of the flitch was a condition of land tenure. That was the case at Wichnor, in Staffordshire, where in Edward III's reign Lord Roger de Somerville held his estate on favourable terms on condition that he did 'maintain and sustain at all times

98. These children are taking part in the Anglican Whit Walk at Manchester.

99. The 600 year-old bottle-kicking scramble, which takes place every Easter Monday at Hallaton, Leicestershire.

00. The bottles re in fact nall wooden asks, two of em filled with eer and the her— aditionally the cond to be opped—a mmy.

101. Distribution of Maundy Money. In the procession, the Queen and clergy carry posies, the traditional protection against fever and plague.

102. (*Above*) The Maundy Money consists of specially minted silver coins to the value of one penny, twopence, threepence and fourpence, of the same size as those minted in the reign of Charles II.

103. The famous Tichborne Dole. The flour is issued from an enormous bin on the steps of Tichborne House by the head of the Tichborne family.

104. In Berkshire, the Ufton Dole is still distributed to the 'poore of Ufton' from a hall window of Ufton Court on a movable date 'about the middle of Lent'.
105. The Biddenden Dole was instituted under the terms of the will of Biddenden maids, Eliza and Mary Chaulkhurst, Siamese twins who were joined together at hip and shoulder.
106. At St Michael's Church, Bristol, on Easter Tuesday, buns known as '2d. starvers' are issued to 500 children.

107. A throw of dice decides the recipient of John How's Charity at Guildford, Surrey.

108. A horn of ale and a small square of bread are still given to any traveller who asks for the Wayfarer's Dole at the Hospital of St Cross, Winchester.

109. (*Right*) At St Bartholomew's the Great, Smithfield, 21 sixpences are given to 21 poor widows every Good Friday under the terms of the Butterworth Charity. The coins are placed on a tombstone in the churchyard and each widow kneels by the stone to pick up her sixpence. She then walks over the stone and is given a hot cross bun and half a crown.

110. The Dunmow Flitch. In this Essex town, a trial is conducted, on mock legal lines, to decide the happiest married couple—the winners receive a flitch of bacon.
111. The Verderers' Court of Swainmote at Lyndhurst, Hampshire. The duties of the New Forest Verderers lie in regulating the exercise of common rights and looking after the commoners' animals through their officers, the agisters, who regularly patrol the Forest.

112. The Court of Purbeck Marblers. This picture shows an apprentice making the run—with a quart of beer in his hand—from the Inn to the Town Hall as quarrymen attempt to snatch it away.

113. The oldest surviving industrial courts in England are the great Barmote Courts that still regulate the lead-mining industry in the Peak District of Derbyshire.

114. Pie Poudre Court, Bristol. For the duration of the fair, the ordinary courts of law used to be suspended and these 'courts of the dusty feet' had jurisdiction over what happened within its precincts.

115. At Kingsteignton Fair, Devon, the decorated carcase of a lamb is carried in procession through the streets every Whit Monday and is afterwards roasted in the open air.

116. The Ebernoe Horn Fair, Sussex. On St James's Day, 25th July, a horned sheep is roasted whole in a pit of embers with the head projecting over the end so that the horns remain undamaged.

117. A scramble for hot pennies follows the traditional readin of the scroll of proclamation of the fair and market at Broughton-in-Furness Lancashire.

118. Horses and ponies stand patientl while waiting to be sold at the Horse Fair at Barnet, Hertfordshire.

f the year but in Lent, a Bacon Flitch hanging in his Hall' to be given,
nder certain conditions 'to every Man and Woman that is married, after
year and a day that their marriage is past'.

Any married couple from any part of England could claim the Dun-
now Flitch. All they had to do then was to go to Little Dunmow Priory
nd, kneeling before the Prior on two stones, solemnly take an oath chant-
d to them by the monks. In its later form it ran:

> You shall swear by Custom of Confession
> That you ne'er made Nuptial Transgression;
> Nor since you were married Man and Wife,
> By Household Brawls or Contentious Strife,
> Or otherwise in Bed or at Board,
> Offended each other in deed or word;
> Or in a Twelve month time and a day,
> Repented not in Thought anyway;
> Or since the Church clerk said Amen,
> Wish'd yourselves unmarried again,
> But continued true and in desire,
> As when you join'd hands in holy Choir.

After the oath had been taken and the bacon awarded, the happy
couple and the bacon were chaired through the village.

After the suppression of the Augustinian Priory, the remains of which
are incorporated in the present parish church, the flitch continued to be
awarded from time to time from Priory Place, though it is significant that
only the successful husband's name was recorded before the 18th century.
In a man's world nobody was very concerned about the wife's happiness.

The successful claimant in 1751, when William Hogarth was present,
cut his bacon up into slices and sold it to make a handsome profit. That
was the last award from Little Dunmow. The next claimant, in 1772, was
turned away by the lord of the manor, and several attempts to revive the
custom were unsuccessful.

Nothing more was heard of the Dunmow Flitch until in 1841 it was
offered to Queen Victoria and the Prince Consort and graciously refused.
About the same time, Harrison Ainsworth published his novel *The Flitch
of Bacon*, which aroused such interest that the custom was revived in
Great Dunmow town hall in 1855 with Ainsworth himself as judge.

After that the trial was held frequently, becoming an annual event from
1890. During the Second World War it was kept going by gifts of flitches

of bacon from Commonwealth countries. Today the judge and jury a
robed, and the trial is conducted on mock legal lines with much tradition
ritual (Plate 110).

Though the Dunmow court may provide little more than a com
interlude, there are still ancient courts that meet for more serious purpose
More than 80 manorial courts in England still sit to discuss the administra
tion of common land and other property. Some have magnificent name
like the Court of the View of Frank Pledge and Court Baron of the Bur
gesses of the Manor of Lichfield, which sits annually on April 23rd, b
they all fit under the broad heading of courts leet or courts baron. Cour
leet, believed to have come with the Norman Conquest, still have th
power to enquire into felonies, though no longer to punish them; cour
baron are purely manorial courts. Ashburton, in Devon, is probabl
unique in having both.

Some of these courts meet infrequently, like the Court Leet of th
Manor of Balneath, in Sussex, which sat in 1959 after a lapse of 46 year
but more of them meet at least annually, as many of them may well hav
done for more than 900 years. The records of the Court Leet of South
ampton are complete from 1550 and go back spasmodically to 1397.

But these courts do not meet merely to maintain an ancient custom
Most of them usually have more important business to transact. Muc
responsibility rests, for instance, on the court leet in the Nottinghamshir
village of Laxton, for farming in the parish is still carried out on the ancien
open field system, and the court, when it meets in the autumn, has no
only to settle demarcation and other disputes, but also to determine agricul
tural policy over the next year. A jury of freeholders inspects the newl
sown wheat, checks the boundaries of the strips and looks out for example
of slovenly husbandry. The court then imposes any fines that may b
necessary before going on to appoint manorial officers.

The titles of such officers vary from place to place, but most of them
come straight out of the Middle Ages. Bailiffs, reeves, haywards and pinder
(or pinners) are common enough. Hungerford's Tutti-men are probabl
unique, but bread weighers, pig drivers, scavengers and ale tasters (o
conners) all turn up in a few places. The ale tasters at Ashburton visit al
the inns of the town once a year to taste the ale. Whenever it is satisfactor
a sprig of evergreen is given to the landlord to hang over his door.

The lord of the manor or his steward usually presides over the court
At Lichfield the town clerk presides as Steward of the Manor and juror
are drawn from the freeholders. The Court Leet of the Royal Manor o

Portland has a jury of 24, but twelve is a more usual number. The Court Baron of Painswick has three jurymen from the commoners of the four parishes that make up the manor, Sheepscombe, Edge, Slad and Painswick. Sickness is normally the only excuse accepted for absence from a jury. A few years ago a juror at Portland was fined £10 for refusing to take the oath. Jurors usually get a free lunch as a reward for their attendance. At Laxton a new juryman pays for the beer at lunch, a custom known as 'tailing the new juror'.

Perhaps even older than the manorial courts is the Court of Swaincote and Attachment of the New Forest, better known as the Verderers' Court, which claims to be the oldest court in England, with the possible exception of the coroner's court. It is composed of ten Verderers—one, the official Verderer, appointed by the Queen, four appointed by such bodies as the Forestry Commission and the Council for the Preservation of Rural England that are interested in the administration of the Forest, and five elected by the commoners of the Forest. The elected Verderers must each hold at least one acre of land with common rights over the Forest. The duties of the Verderers lie in regulating the exercise of common rights and looking after the commoners' animals through their officers, the agisters, who regularly patrol the Forest, for the Forestry Commission, who otherwise control the New Forest, have little to do with the animals.

The court meets at roughly six-weekly intervals and is open to the public. It is held in the Verderers' Hall in the Queen's House at Lyndhurst, on the busy Southampton–Bournemouth main road. It is a moment of curious paradox when, with traffic swirling past outside, the senior agister rises in the dock and with his right hand raised proclaims in the age-old manner: 'Oyez! Oyez! Oyez! All manner of persons who have any presentment or matter or thing to do at this Court of Swaincote let him come forward and he shall be heard! God Save the Queen!' The rest of the proceedings are less formal. Commoners with complaints make presentments which the Verderers listen to and discuss before giving a ruling (Plate 111).

The Verderers' Court of Attachment in the Forest of Dean is kept rather less busy, mainly because there are fewer animals to deal with in Dean than in the New Forest. The court is scheduled to meet every 40 days, but most of the meetings are formally adjourned in the absence of any business and in practice it sits nowadays about once a year when matters concerning the Forest are discussed with the deputy surveyor, who is the local representative of the Forestry Commission. The court still has powers to try offences against the vert and venison—that is against the growing trees and plants and against the beasts of the Forest—and against encroachment, but nowadays the Forestry Commission usually prosecute such offenders in the ordinary courts of law.

The present duties of the Verderers are mainly administrative. They act as intermediaries between the Forestry Commission and the local people, and also keep a watchful eye on the amenities of the Forest. There are only four of them, as there have been since the office of verderer was instituted, probably in the reign of Canute (c. 1016–35). Since the 17th century their court has met in the beautiful, lonely, Speech House, in the heart of the Forest.

A curious water-borne court of less ancient vintage is the Admiralty Court of the City of Rochester, established under an Act of Parliament of 1729 'for regulating, well-ordering, Governing and Improving the Oyster Fishery in the River Medway and waters thereof', which meets annually in early July in a decorated barge moored off the end of Rochester pier. The mayor, as Admiral of the Medway, presides over a court of city aldermen and a jury composed of freemen of the river. The court's duties are concerned purely with the administration of the oyster fishing.

Mention was made in Chapter Ten of the Court of Purbeck Marblers, which meets on Shrove Tuesday in Corfe Castle town hall. Its duty is to elect wardens and stewards for the ensuing year and to initiate apprentices. In the initiation ceremony each apprentice buys a quart of beer from the Fox Inn and tries to get it across to the town hall while the quarrymen attempt to snatch it away. Those who succeed in reaching their goal with their beer unspilt, and pay their initiation fees, become freemen of the Company of Purbeck Marblers, which has held its court at least since the 17th century and possibly long before that (Plate 112).

But the oldest surviving industrial courts in England are the Great Barmote Courts that still regulate the lead-mining industry in the Peak District of Derbyshire. At the Inquisition of Ashbourne, held in 1288 at the command of Edward I, two such courts were set up: one at Monyash later transferred to Ashford in the Water—for the High Peak, and the other at Wirksworth for the Low Peak. The industry today is at a very low ebb, but the Wirksworth Court still meets twice yearly, in April and October. The Great Barmote Court for the Joint Liberty of Stoney Middleton and Eyam sits annually, usually in May (Plate 113).

The duty of these courts has always been to see that justice is done between 'Kyng and minour, and between minour and minour'. The

ndustry is traditionally open to all comers, and any man who discovers a
vein of ore has the right to work it, subject to certain conditions. One of
the main duties of the courts is confirming or vetoing the claims of
prospectors, though such claims are fairly rare nowadays. Before the pass-
ng of the Derbyshire Mining Customs and Mineral Courts Act of 1852
these courts could pass what was virtually a sentence of death on miners
caught stealing ore from the mines. These powers were referred to in a
long poem written by Edward Manlove, a steward of the Wirksworth
Court, in 1663:

> For stealing oar twice from the minery,
> The Thief that's taken fined twice shall be,
> But the third time, that he commits such theft,
> Shall have a knife stuck through his hand to the 'Haft
> Into the Stow, and there till death shall stand,
> Or loose himself by cutting loose his hand;
> And shall forswear the franchise of that mine,
> And always lose his freedom from that time.

The business of the courts is conducted by the Steward, who is a solicitor,
and the Queen's Barmaster, who looks after the Queen's interests in the
mining-fields, assisted by a grand jury. The procedure follows a long-
established pattern. On arrival, the grand jurymen are regaled with bread
and cheese, beer and tobacco at a near-by inn. This is a relic of the days
when they had a long walk over the bleak hills to reach the court-room.
The refreshments disposed of, the Barmaster reads the proclamation
summoning the court. The Steward then swears in the jurymen and
reminds them of their responsibilities and the need for strict impartiality
in carrying out the customs of the mines and enforcing the laws.

After a further proclamation inviting the raising of any matters re-
quiring the attention of the court, the Barmaster presents his statement of
the quantity and value of the ore mined within the jurisdiction of the court
and reports the amounts paid in royalties and tithes. When the business is
over the court adjourns for a dinner provided by the Lord of the Mineral
Field, after which punch is drunk, and tobacco smoked in long clay pipes.
The jury is not discharged, but is liable to be called on for its judgments
any time during the following six or twelve months.

The Low Peak Barmote Court meets in the Moot Hall at Wirksworth.
The building itself dates only from 1814, but it contains an oblong brass
dish, to hold fourteen pints, that was used as a standard measure for lead

ore. It was made, according to the inscription round the rim, 'in the III year of the reign of King Henry VIII, before George, Earle of Shrowes bury', and was to remain in the Moot Hall, 'so as the Merchauntes o mynours may resorte to the same at all tymes to make the true measur after the same'.

CHAPTER FOURTEEN

Fairs and Wakes

A number of ancient courts still exist in London and some provincial cities, and a few of these remain active in hearing civil actions. One of them is Bristol's Tolzey Court, which has unlimited civil jurisdiction in the area, and attached to it is a Court of Pie Poudre, perhaps the only surviving example of the courts that used to dispense instant justice on the fairgrounds of England.

For the duration of the fair the ordinary courts of law were suspended and these 'courts of the dusty feet'—of the wandering chapmen who frequented the fairs—had jurisdiction over what happened within its precincts. Such courts, with the ability to act quickly, were necessary when most of the traders were itinerant, but their importance declined together with the importance of fairs, and most of them lapsed after the County Courts Act of 1888. But somehow the Bristol court has survived to be opened outside the Stag and Hounds Inn in Old Market Street at 10 a.m. every September 30th by the Sergeant-at-Mace and then adjourned to the Tolzey Court (Plate 114).

Courts of pie-powder came in with the Normans, who first granted charters for fairs, but the shadowy pre-history of the fair goes back much further than that; further indeed than the beginnings of the English nation. Their origins were probably bound up with long-forgotten pagan festivals, for before the trading element was introduced festivals were what—now the wheel has turned full circle—they have become again. The very name comes from the Latin *feria*, a holiday. The Christian Church took over these festivities; there would be festivals to coincide with the anniversary of the saint to whom the parish church was dedicated. People flocked to hear Mass and stayed to join in the fun of games and dancing. Traders set up booths and stalls in the churchyard, a custom that the law stopped in 1448.

After the Norman Conquest many fairs were started by royal charter and many existing ones legalised, including some that were said to have been started by Alfred the Great. Nearly 5,000 such charters were granted between 1200 and 1400, mostly to powerful landowners or to great religious houses. Trade, both wholesale and retail, became the prime purpose of fairs; the fun was secondary.

Thus our fairs fall into two categories: the trading fairs established by royal charter, of which Sturbridge Fair, near Cambridge, described by Defoe as 'not only the greatest in the whole nation, but in the world', was the classic example, and those that sprang up to mark a church's patronal festival and ought correctly to be called 'wakes', as indeed they often are. Of this latter class the largest survivor is probably St Giles' Fair at Oxford, which has outlived the city's four charter fairs. It originated in the annual wake festival of Walton parish and still occupies its original site in St Giles and Magdalen Street in the manor of Walton outside the city walls.

Of the charter fairs, one of which gave its name to London's fashionable district of Mayfair, that at St Ives, in Huntingdonshire, is among the most interesting historically. It dates from a charter granted in 1110 by Henry I to St Benedict of Ramsey and St Ive of Slepe, and is especially remarkable in being older than the town. Indeed the town owes its existence to the fair. St Ive was a Persian bishop buried at Slepe. When Abbot Ednoth moved the saint's bones to Ramsey Abbey a subordinate house and church were established near the site and dedicated to St Ive. There the fair dedicated to the saint was held in Easter Week, lasting at first for eight days, but being later extended to the 40 days before Pentecost. Trading was carried out from houses as well as from booths, and these houses became the nucleus of the pleasant riverside town of St Ives. In the 13th century the fair became one of the most important in England, but it declined during the Hundred Years' War, and today there is merely a one-day pleasure fair in October and a market on Whit Monday.

There are even older charter fairs than the one at St Ives; Barton Fair at Tewkesbury has been held on October 10th since the end of the 11th century. Originally held at the gates of the monastery, it moved out into the town streets when the gates were demolished in 1651. The Sloe Fair at Chichester has been held on the Feast of St Faith (October 6th) since 1108. Originally the Bishop's Fair, it takes its present name from an ancient sloe tree in Oatlands Park, where it is always held.

Summercourt Fair, the oldest charter fair in Cornwall, may be older than either of them, and Weyhill Fair, in Hampshire, where in Cobbett's time the turnover in sheep amounted to £300,000 and where Hardy set his wife-sale in the *Mayor of Casterbridge*, certainly was older until it petered out recently. It had been held on the same hill-top site on a cross-roads at the boundary of three parishes at least since the 11th century and it may have gone back much further than that. The discovery of ox-teeth and other relics hereabouts suggests that it was the site of pagan sacrifice and festival. Further weight to this theory is lent by the old custom that used to be observed here of 'horning the colt', at which any newcomer to the fair underwent an initiation ceremony in the village inn while wearing a cap fitted with a pair of ram's horns, which still hang in the Star Inn. Here, as at Abbots Bromley, the horns may have some ancient ritual significance, going back perhaps to the time when animals were sacrified and their heads cut off and struggled for.

This concern for the heads of animals crops up in several places. At Westhoughton, in Lancashire, a huge communal pie used to be made in the shape of a cow's head during the Wakes Week that begins on St Bartholomew's Day, the patronal festival of the parish church. Nowadays this pie is more often replaced by numerous small pasties, but Westhoughton people are still nicknamed Keaw-Yeds (cow-heads). A local theory that the tradition began when a farmer cut off the head of a cow that was trapped in a gate is now discredited, for the incident, which has some factual basis, took place about 1908 and the tradition is far older. A more acceptable theory associates it with St Bartholomew, who was the patron saint of butchers, but it seems still more likely that it goes back with other traditions concerned with animals' heads to pagan times, and has close affinities with the Ebernoe Horn Fair, in Sussex, and the Kingsteignton Ram-roasting Fair, in Devon.

At Ebernoe, on St James's Day (July 25th), a horned sheep is roasted whole in a pit of embers with the head projecting over the end so that the horns remain undamaged. The sheep is decapitated when cooked, the mutton being eaten at lunch by the players in an annual cricket match and the head being awarded to the winning side to hang in their local pub (Plate 116). At the Kingsteignton Fair, a much older festival than the neighbouring and better known Widecombe Fair, the decorated carcase of a lamb is carried in procession through the streets every Whit Monday and is afterwards roasted in the open air, sports being held while it is cooking. Here the local tradition is that the lamb-roasting arose from a pagan sacrifice in thanksgiving for the gift of water. A spring is supposed to have emerged in a meadow after prayers had been offered to the gods and it has never since dried up (Plate 115).

A deer is roasted at Cranham Feast, high above Gloucester, on the second Monday in August, when a lunch for residents and guests, a fancy-dress parade, sports and an annual tug-of-war between Cranham and Upton St Leonards supplement the usual fun-fair. Until 1964, when traffic dislocation compelled a move to a field in another part of the parish, the feast was always held on common land in Cranham Woods, adjoining the A46 trunk road, and it is thought locally that it originated at some unspecified date when villagers asserted their right to common land by roasting a deer on it in the presence of the lord of the manor. But here again a pagan origin seems likely.

It has been suggested that the Lichfield Greenhill Bower started as a pagan floral rite, though local opinion links its origin with King Oswy of Northumberland, who founded a bishopric at Lichfield about 656, after his conquest of Mercia. A procession of the various craft guilds was a feature of the Bower in the Middle Ages, and, though today it is chiefly a sports and pleasure fair, a procession with floral decorations still takes place. The Bower, held on Whit Monday, has become mixed up with the Court of Arraye of Men and Arms, a ceremony that must go back to the Statute of Winchester of 1285, when it became compulsory for every freeman between the ages of fifteen and sixty to equip himself for war and to present his weapons and armour for periodic inspection. Although the courts of array ceased to be necessary in the reign of James I, Lichfield has refused to be stampeded into a dissolution of its ancient court.

Another medieval survival is the custom still followed at several fairs of displaying a hand or glove as a symbol that visiting merchants might enter the town and that all might trade there without fear of arrest or punishment so long as the charter was respected. The glove is displayed at Exeter's Lammas Fair, now held on the Tuesday before the third Wednesday in July, and at the Barnstaple September Fair, where the proclamation is read by the town clerk from the steps of Queen's Walk and repeated at the town's ancient gates. At Honiton Fair, which dates from 1257 and is held on the Tuesday and Wednesday after July 19th, a gilt glove is carried on the top of a decorated staff by the town crier, who proclaims: 'Oyez! Oyez! Oyez! The glove is up! The glove is up! The Fair is open! God save the Queen!' Hot pennies are then thrown to scrambling children from the windows of the main inns. A similar scramble for hot pennies follows the traditional reading of the scroll of proclamation of

Broughton-in-Furness fair and market, which dates from 1593 (Plate 117).

A most unusual custom connected with Sherborne's Pack Monday Fair, which takes place on the Monday after Old Michaelmas Day (October 10th), is threatened with extinction. Soon after midnight a band of young people used to march through the streets banging tin cans and dustbin lids and blowing bugles, horns and whistles in an ear-bursting cacophony. The 'musicians' called themselves Teddy Roe's Band. The original Teddy Roe was reputedly the late-15th-century foreman mason of Sherborne Abbey. The story goes that when the fan-vaulting in the Abbey was completed in 1490, the workmen packed up their tools—which explains the name Pack Monday—and were then led by Teddy Roe in a noisy march of triumph through the streets. But it has also been suggested that the custom began much earlier with the noises made to frighten away evil spirits from a pagan festival. Numerous attempts have been made to silence Teddy Roe's Band, and in 1964 and 1965 the police suppressed it because of increasing hooliganism.

Attempts to put a stop to the ancient two-day charter fair at Yarm, in north Yorkshire, in October, have so far come to nothing. Opponents of this last of the town's four fairs, which dates from a charter of King John in 1216, claim that it brings 'undesirable elements' to the town, fouls the streets and disorganises traffic. Although it is now principally a pleasure fair, the sale of horses for which it is traditionally famous has not entirely ceased, and it may still be possible in the main street of Yarm to see two gypsies striking a bargain in the old way by slapping hands.

Horse fairs generally are not quite what they were, but Stow-on-the-Wold still manages to fill its spacious market-square with animals and buyers on May 9th and October 24th each year. Stow Fair, founded by a charter of Edward IV in 1476, began as a sheep fair, but changed over to horses when the great wool trade of the Cotswolds declined. Crowds still flock to the horse fairs at Barnet and Brough and to Bampton Pony Fair, in Devon, while even a village as small as Belton, near Loughborough, maintains a June horse fair whose charter dates from 1234, though in recent years the number of horses in the village street has fallen to a mere 40 or so (Plate 118).

Most other specialised fairs have degenerated into pleasure fairs. Nottingham's Goose Fair, on the first Thursday in October and the two following days, may still be the largest fair in the Midlands, but it is no longer the mart for the sale of 20,000 geese or more, as it was in the Middle Ages, when it lasted for 21 days (Plate 119).

The great Mop fairs continue to flourish at Stratford-on-Avon and elsewhere in the West Midlands, but they have long ceased to be hiring fairs. These Mops began after the Black Death in the middle of the fourteenth century when there was an acute shortage of labour in agriculture. A law of that time required every able-bodied man to offer himself for hire at a fixed wage. An Act of 1563 confirmed, strengthened and extended this law.

But why Mop? Some authorities believe it comes from the Latin *mappa*, meaning 'public games', but the more popular and probably correct version is that it comes simply from the mop that girls carried to indicate that they were looking for work in domestic service, for all those seeking employment wore some emblem of their trade. The shepherd's hat bore a lock of wool; the milkmaids wore a tuft of cowhair.

By law the hiring was for one calendar year, but in some places it was for only 51 weeks. This was a crafty move to prevent an unemployed person from getting a settlement in a parish and becoming a burden on the local poor rate. The unwritten contract started from the moment that a coin was pressed into the worker's hand. This was the hiring penny, or God's penny, which the inflationary spiral had pushed up to one shilling by the 19th century.

Not all servants—or employers, for that matter—obtained a good bargain. So a second fair, called a Runaway Mop, was held in some places about a fortnight after the first. Some of these Runaway Mops survive, in name only, especially in the West Midlands.

The decline of the hiring fair as such dates from the 1860s when an agitation began for their suppression on the grounds that such fairs had become 'drunken orgies'. In response to this clamour, 'Servants' Registration Offices' were set up in most market-towns. The establishment of Labour Exchanges in 1909 was the last nail in the coffin of the old hiring fairs in their traditional form.

The character of the North Country wakes has changed too. From a one-day fair linked with the patronal festival of the parish church it developed in the 19th century into a week's unpaid holiday, when all the mills in a town shut down and the machinery could be overhauled. Now it has grown into a fortnight's paid holiday during which not only mills, but most other industries and many shops close. The workpeople prefer it to staggered holidays, and the shopkeepers are happy because they can put up their shutters and go away without losing trade.

Another characteristically northern custom, especially popular in ancashire and the West Riding, is the Walking Day, on which the ongregations of churches of all denominations walk in procession through he streets of their town. Many of these processions of witness, which are roducts of the first half of the 19th century, are held at Whitsuntide, but Warrington's Walk Day, a public holiday in the town, is held on the Friay nearest July 1st.

Club walking is another 19th-century tradition that has survived nainly in northern England. Members of benefit clubs, trading associaions and the like turn out in full force in their best clothes to parade hrough the streets, usually ending their walk at the parish church for a hort service, followed by a meal in some public hall.

A few of these clubs are for women only, having been founded during he Napoleonic Wars, when many of the men were away fighting. One at Neston, in the Wirral, has operated since 1814, paying out sickness and death benefits among its hundred or so members whenever necessary. On the first Thursday in June its members meet at the church school, whose children are given a holiday for the occasion, to walk in procession to the parish church. The procession is a colourful one led by a band and followed by the choir, clergy, civic dignitaries and young girls and adult members, each carrying a stave wrapped in silver foil or white cloth with its top garlanded with freshly cut flowers. After the service, during which the garlands are placed at the ends of the pews, a second procession walks round the parish to the cross, where another service is held, followed by tea in a neighbouring hall (Plate 120).

The even older Baschurch Ladies' Club, formed as the Baschurch Female Friendly Society in 1802, has its anniversary 'Walk' as near as possible to June 24th, when its members go in procession to the parish church carrying wands decorated with flowers. On reaching the church, the ladies form an archway with their wands. After a special service they march again through the quiet Shropshire village.

CHAPTER FIFTEEN

All Manner of Customs

When an old custom dies in England it is often because it has been replaced by a new one. Thus the Halloween fires, damped down by the influence of the Reformation, burst out anew on November 5th as Guy Fawkes Night celebrations. Only in this way can one account for the continued popularity in an age of religious tolerance, or apathy, of a custom that was originally imposed by Act of Parliament.

In the old Celtic calendar October 31st was New Year's Eve, the eve of winter and of the Feast of the Dead when gods and spirits walked abroad and the dead returned to earth. Household fires were extinguished and relit later from the flames of the bonfires that welcomed the returning spirits. Men carried burning brands out to the fields and spread the ashes over the land to fertilise the soil.

The Christian Church, finding the custom too deeply rooted to be eradicated, compromised in 837 by establishing November 1st as the Feast of All Saints and by fixing the Feast of All Souls on November 2nd in 998. Although Protestant England frowned on Halloween fires as smacking of Popery as well as an excuse for rowdiness, the tradition persisted on the Celtic fringe and in the north until well into the 19th century. Mischief Night in Yorkshire, when young men indulge in licensed vandalism by removing gates and other readily portable property, is almost certainly a carry over from the sort of merriment that accompanied the bonfires. Mischief Night, along with the bonfires, has now been transferred to November 4th, but in some areas it is still remembered by old people as an alternative name for Halloween. In other districts May Eve, another important pagan date, was Mischief Night (Plate 121).

In most parts of the country Guy Fawkes Night provided a perfect excuse for lighting bonfires and having fun on a perfectly respectable—

and indeed legally enforceable—pretext in place of an old, but tarnished custom. In some places, moreover, there were particular reasons why the burning in effigy of Guy Fawkes, as a symbol of Roman Catholicism, should be enjoyed with special relish. At Lewes seventeen people, mostly simple village folk whose crime had been to read the Bible for themselves, were burnt at the stake in the market-place during the Marian persecutions. Six men and four women perished together in one fire in 1557. It is hardly surprising, then, to find that Lewes still celebrates Bonfire Night with considerable gusto (Plate 122).

The festivities are organised by six Bonfire Societies whose members are known as Bonfire Boys. They used to light their bonfires in the streets, much to the consternation of the authorities, who were also worried by the practice of rolling lighted tar barrels about the place. The police made several attempts to stop the celebrations, without doing more than provoke fairly serious riots. Eventually a happy compromise was reached that allowed the bonfires to go on so long as the societies accepted responsibility for their orderly conduct.

Nowadays members of each society march to an open place outside the town to burn their effigy, which is usually filled with fireworks. But this, the climax of the evening, does not come much before midnight. The proceedings start around 5.30 with each society marching in procession to the War Memorial, where wreaths are laid in memory of fallen Bonfire Boys and a short address and a hymn follow. The Cliffe Society, which still possesses an 18th-century banner bearing the words 'No Popery', uses a Bonfire prayer which is also over 200 years old. Throughout the evening there are torchlight processions through the town.

Other Sussex towns and villages celebrate Guy Fawkes Night with similar enthusiasm. Rye has a 'Rye Fawkes', with a visiting 'personality' to light its bonfire, and burns a boat, among other things. Battle has a torchlight procession, followed by a spectacular firework display in front of the historic abbey. Such celebrations spill over the county boundary into Kent, where at Edenbridge three brass bands take part in the torchlight procession of decorated floats. And in the West Country young men do incredibly dangerous things with blazing tar barrels at Ottery St Mary, Devon (Plate 123). Bridgwater celebrates the occasion with equal enthusiasm, but on the nearest Thursday to Bonfire Night. Shopkeepers thus have time on their early-closing day to board up their windows before the fireworks go off.

An echo of the first Guy Fawkes Night in 1605 is the inspection of the

Houses of Parliament by Yeomen of the Guard on the morning of the State Opening of Parliament. Armed with lanterns, the Yeomen search the cellars. When they are satisfied that no intruder is lurking there and that no explosives have been planted, a message is sent that the Queen and Parliament may safely assemble.

Guy Fawkes Night is not the only occasion when ceremonial bonfires are lit in England. The Northumberland village of Whalton lights one on old Midsummer Eve (July 4th) on the village green. When darkness falls the fire is lit and the children dance round it in a ring. After that there is dancing to the music of a fiddle and scrambling for sweets by the children.

This custom can be traced back to the pagan festival of the summer solstice, which fell on June 21st, though it was replaced in early Christian times by the Feast of the Nativity of St John the Baptist, three days later. Such fires, still known in Scotland as Beltane Fires, were lit in honour of the sun god.

Since the 1920s, when the Federation of Old Cornwall Societies revived the ancient custom, a chain of bonfires has blazed out across the whole length of Cornwall on St John's Eve, although in recent years sentries have had to be posted to prevent vandals from prematurely lighting the fires. When the St Ives beacon was lit too soon in 1958, the *Guardian* reported that a team of volunteers, including the mayor, cut fir trees and built a second fire to save the tradition.

The speaking that accompanies the ceremony of lighting the fires is in the Cornish language. After the fire has been blessed, the master of ceremonies chants:—

> *Now set the pyre*
> *At once on fire,*
> *Let flames aspire*
> *In God's high name!*

A Lady of the Flowers then throws wild flowers and herbs on to the fire, with the words:—

> *In one bunch together bound*
> *Flowers for burning here are found,*
> *Both good and ill;*
> *Thousandfold let good seed spring,*
> *Wicked weeds, fast withering.*

When the fire is burning, young couples sometimes follow the old tradition of jumping hand in hand through the flames to bring themselves

119. Nottingham Goose Fair, like many other specialised fairs, has become a pleasure fair. The illuminated stalls and entertainments stand out against the dark sky in this picture.

120. Club walking is a tradition that has survived mainly in northern England. On Ladies Day at Neston, Cheshire, a colourful procession, led by a band and followed by the choir, clergy, civic dignitaries, young girls and adult members, each carrying a stave with its top garlanded with freshly cut flowers, may be seen entering the church.

121. Mischief Night in Leeds. A home-made lantern lights the way for a girl to put syrup on unsuspecting people's door handles. 122. The people of Lewes, Sussex, still celebrate Bonfire Night with enthusiasm. Here we see a Guy Fawkes being erected.

123. In Ott␣ Mary, Dev␣ young men␣ incredibly␣ dangerous␣ with blazi␣ barrels on␣ Night.

124. The custom of rolling brightly coloured eggs down a hillside is still followed at Avenham Park, Preston, Lancashire.
125. Apple Wassailing is still carried on at Carhampton, near Minehead, Somerset, on Old Twelfth Night, 17th January. 126. On St Martin's Day, 11th November, every year, six Fenny Poppers—little cannons, each seven inches high and weighing about 20 pounds—are fired at Fenny Stratford, Buckinghamshire.

127. The medieval Mystery Plays of York have been revived and are performed at the city's festival every third year.

128. Within the last few years the villagers of Leusdon, Devon, have abandoned their ancient practice of rolling a cartwheel down the slopes of Mel Tor on the eve of St John the Baptist Day.

ood luck. The ashes of the fire are preserved in sacks and used to form the oundations of the following year's beacon.

The bonfire that is lit at St Cleer, near Liskeard, on the same evening, as a different purpose. Crowned with a witch's broom and hat, it is lesigned to keep witches away for the year. An oak sickle, newly cut, is lways thrown into the flames. This may be a symbol of the human acrifice that was once offered to keep evil spirits away. There are records s late as 1800—with later hearsay evidence—of Cornish farmers sacrificng young calves in bonfires for that purpose.

The New Year's Eve bonfire at Allendale, in Northumberland, probably has its origin in the celebration of the winter solstice and the first igns of returning life. It is lit at midnight after young men in fancy dress ave paraded through the parish with wooden tubs of burning tar on their eads. The people dance round it before the men go off to let in the New Year in the traditional manner known as first-footing, which is still popular in Scotland and nothern England.

The first-footer—the first person to enter a house in the New Year— hould be a dark man, preferably a stranger. On no account should he ave auburn hair, a squint, flat feet or meeting eyebrows. Entering the ouse in silence, he should put a piece of coal on the fire, eat bread or cake nd drink wine or whisky to ensure an adequate supply of fuel, food and drink throughout the year. This confidence in dark men may indicate that the custom began when the swarthy Celts inhabited these islands.

Yet another custom with pagan origins is that of Apple Wassailing, still carried on at Carhampton, near Minehead, and other West Country villages on Old Twelfth Night (January 17th). The villagers form a circle round the largest apple tree in a selected orchard. Pieces of toast soaked in cider are hung in the branches for the robins, who represent the 'good spirits' of the tree. The leading wassailer utters an incantation and shot-gun volleys are fired through the branches to frighten away the evil spirits (Plate 125). Then the tree is toasted in cider and urged in song to bring forth much fruit. The last verse of the song runs:

> Old Apple tree, old apple tree,
> We've come to wassail thee,
> To bear and to bow apples enow,
> Hats full, caps full, three bushel bags full,
> Barn floors full and a little heap under the stairs.

Many customs at Easter, which takes its name from the Saxon godde
of spring, Eostre, are connected with the egg, the symbol of the life forc
The Bishop and Dean of Chester no longer take eggs into the cathedral an
indulge in egg-throwing matches with the choristers, as they once di
but the custom of rolling brightly coloured eggs down a hillside is sti
followed at Preston, Scarborough, Barton-upon-Humber and elsewher
In medieval times it was said to represent the rolling away of the ston
from Christ's tomb, but the true origin is more likely to be pre-Christia
(Plate 124).

Even Christmas, as a time of public rejoicing, has pre-Christia
beginnings. In the Roman Empire it was a sacred day in honour of th
birth of the Unconquered Sun, as well as the chief festival of Attis, th
Phrygian god, and of Mithras. It fell between the Saturnalia, which laste
a week, and the Kalends of January that began the New Year. It was no
until towards the end of the 4th century that the Christian Church decide
to celebrate the uncertain date of Christ's birth, previously observe
together with the Feast of the Epiphany on January 6th, on Decembe
25th.

It is sometimes suggested that the modern Christmas was the invention
of Charles Dickens, aided by Prince Albert. While this is too sweeping, i
is true that Dickens did much to publicise the festive season, and the Princ
Consort, if he did not in fact introduce the Christmas tree, certainly en
couraged the fashion by installing one at Windsor. But it is only in thi
century that tall lighted trees, imported by special permission as the im-
port of trees is normally forbidden, have appeared in our streets a
Christmas time.

Indeed many of our Christmas customs are comparatively modern.
The first Christmas card dates back only to 1846, and the custom of hanging up stockings on Christmas Eve was unknown before the 19th century
Turkeys were only introduced into this country from the New World ir
the 16th century. Plum pudding, in the form of plum porridge, goes back
a century earlier, and mince-pies are older still.

Most Christmas customs are common to all parts of Britain and need
no further comment here, but Bridgnorth, Salop, has one that is unique
On Boxing Day morning small boys from Low Town go up to High
Town with blackened faces and jackets turned inside out and decorated
with coloured cloth. Each boy carries a broomstick. Working in pairs
they hold mock single-stick contests with the staves, at the same time singing ten verses of the old song that begins 'This old man he played one'.

while money is collected from the spectators. The performance closes promptly at noon. Nobody knows the origin of this custom, which seems to have gone on for centuries.

Some customs defy all attempts at classification. One of these is the ancient Revel at Marhamchurch, near Bude, which commemorates the bringing of Christianity to the village by the Celtic St Marwenne in the 6th century, and is held each year on the Monday after the Feast of St Marwenne (August 12th). A Queen of the Revel is crowned by Father Time, representing St Marwenne, outside the church at the very spot where the saint reputedly had her cell. The Queen then rides through the village behind a brass band and followed by her attendants to the Revel ground, where there are side-shows, stalls, competitions, Cornish wrestling and a Cornish tea for all.

Further east, at Plymouth, the lord mayor leads an annual pilgrimage each June to the Corporation reservoir at Burrator to drink the health of the founder of the city's water supply, Sir Francis Drake (a great-great nephew of the famous admiral), who was Recorder of Plymouth from 1696 to 1717. A goblet of wine is passed round the official party, and each person in turn drinks to 'the pious memory of Sir Francis Drake'. Then the goblet is again passed round and the toast 'May the descendants of him who brought us water never want wine' is drunk.

A noisier celebration takes place each year on St Martin's Day (November 11th) at Fenny Stratford, in Buckinghamshire, when six fenny poppers fire a *feux de joie*, as they have done ever since 1730, when Dr Browne Willis, the antiquary, presented them to the church which he had built in memory of his grandfather. These queer little cannons, each seven inches high and weighing about twenty pounds, are made of forged gun-metal. Loaded with gunpowder and discharged by a red-hot rod applied to the touch-holes, they fire four salvoes at four-hourly intervals from 8 a.m. At other times they are kept padlocked in the belfry of the church, which Dr Browne Willis insisted should be dedicated to St Martin, as he happened to have been born on St Martin's Day in St Martin's Lane, London (Plate 126).

An even more extraordinary custom is observed at Whitby on the day before Ascension Day. It is called the Horngarth, or Planting the Penny Hedge, and the local legend is that the hedge is planted as a penance for a crime committed in 1159 by William de Bruce, Ralph de Percy and a freeholder named Allotson.

The story goes that the three men were hunting in a wood called

Eskdale Side, belonging to the Abbot of Whitby, when they encountered a large wild boar, which the hounds pursued and wounded. Exhausted, the boar took refuge in the cell of a hermit, who shut out the hounds and continued with his devotions. The frustrated hunters burst into the cell and mortally wounded the hermit. But before he died he asked for the men to be brought before him in the presence of the abbot and then begged that their lives might be spared on condition that they performed the annual Horngarth penance and that their descendants were charged with continuing the custom.

At sunrise on Ascension Eve they were to go to Stray-head Wood in Eskdale Side and cut stakes which were to be carried to Whitby harbour and planted there at the water's edge. The stakes were to be cut with a knife of 'a penny price', and throughout the operation of collecting the materials and making the hedge, which had to stand for three tides, the abbot's bailiff had to sound his horn at intervals, proclaim their crime and cry 'Out upon you'.

The legend is sufficiently picturesque to have been used by Sir Walter Scott in *Marmion*, but it seems more likely that the custom, which is still observed in its entirety, started as a condition of land tenure in Saxon times, and that, as in so many places, a story has been made up to fit a custom that could not otherwise be readily explained.

Will customs like this and the others I have mentioned die out as the public becomes more sophisticated? I think not, though inevitably there will be some casualties. Within the last few years the villagers of Leusdon, in Devon, have abandoned their ancient and apparently pointless practice of rolling a cartwheel down the slopes of Mel Tor on the eve of St John the Baptist's Day (Plate 128). Preservationists may deplore the end of this and other customs, but artificial respiration will not keep them alive. A custom will only survive if there is a spontaneous desire by a large body of folk to keep it going.

But that desire is usually there, and it is often encouraged by modern methods of publicity. The well-dresser at Tissington who was proud that well-dressing had made the village famous was expressing a view shared in other places where old customs have received wide publicity on the radio and television, as well as in articles and books.

And sometimes a custom that has apparently died out will spring to life again. The Dunmow Flitch trial, the Olney Pancake Race and the medieval mystery plays of York, performed at the city's festival every third year, are three examples among many (Plate 127).

New customs, too, emerge almost unnoticed. 'We haven't any old customs here so we thought we'd start one', somebody in the Derbyshire village of Walton-on-Trent was reported to have said in replying to a question about the origin of the 'conker' championship which has now become an annual event in the village. On a national scale, the Battle of Britain fly-past and the London-to-Brighton veteran car run are two examples of embryonic customs.

Above all, the inborn conservatism of the English people is the best defender of our old customs. We as a nation—and this is as often a vice as a virtue—do not welcome change, and will often go to great lengths to resist it. Mrs Woolley who (as recorded in Chapter Ten) frustrated an attempt to stamp out Shrovetide football at Ashbourne and the Bonfire Boys of Lewes would have gone to prison rather than lose their old customs. Their successors are not likely to give them up any more lightly.

Abridged Bibliography

Addison, W. *English Fairs and Markets*: Batsford, 1953.
Alford, V. *Sword Dance and Drama*: Merlin Press, 1962.
Berry, C. *Portrait of Cornwall*: Robert Hale, 1963.
Brett, H. *English Myths and Traditions*: Batsford, 1952.
Chambers, Sir E. K. *The English Folk Play*: Clarendon Press, Oxford, 1933.
Chambers, Sir E. K. *The Medieval Stage*: 2 vols., Clarendon Press, Oxford, 1903.
Crawford, P. *In England Still*: Arrowsmith, 1938.
Ditchfield, P. H. *Old English Customs*: G. Redway, 1896.
Drabble, P. *Staffordshire*: Robert Hale, 1948.
Drake-Carnell, F. J. *Old English Customs*: Batsford, 1938.
Frazer, Sir J. G. *The Golden Bough*: Macmillan, 1936.
ed. Gomme, G. L. *Popular Superstitions and Traditions*: Ellis Stock, 1887.
Hole, C. *Christmas and its Customs*: Richard Bell, 1957.
Hole, C. *English Customs and Usage*: Batsford, 1950.
Howard, A. *Endless Cavalcade*: Arthur Barker, 1964.
Hunt, C. *British Customs and Traditions*: Ernest Benn, 1954.
James, E. O. *Seasonal Feasts and Festivals*: Thames and Hudson, 1961.
Krappe, A. H. *The Science of Folklore*: Methuen, 1930.
Long, G. *The Folklore Calendar*: Philip Allan, 1930.
Muncey, R. W. L. *Old English Fairs*: Sheldon Press, 1936.
ed. Plomer, W. *Kilvert's Diary 1870-79*: Jonathan Cape, 1944.
Porteous, C. *The Beauty and Mystery of Well-Dressing*: Pilgrim Press, Derby, 1949.
Porteous, C. *The Ancient Customs of Derbyshire*: The Derbyshire Countryside, Derby, 1962.
Price, N. *Pagan's Progress*: Museum Press, 1954.
Tiddy, R. J. E. *The Mummer's Play*: Clarendon Press, Oxford, 1923.
Whistler, L. *The English Festivals*: Heinemann, 1947.
Wright, A. R. *British Calendar Customs*: 3 vols., publ. for the Folk-Lore Society, William Glasher, 1936-38.
Wymer, N. *A Breath of England*: Lutterworth Press, 1948.
Wymer, N. *Mere and Moorland*: Lutterworth Press, 1951.

ABRIDGED BIBLIOGRAPHY

MAGAZINES

Folklore: Journal of the Folk-Lore Society, London.

Journal of the English Folk Dance and Song Society: London.

I have also consulted numerous general, regional and county histories; magazines additional to those mentioned above; pamphlets, guide-books and newspapers.

Topographical Index

(The figures in bold type refer to plate numbers)